FRANCIS FRITH'S

ST NEOTS - A HISTORY & CELEBRATION

THE FRANCIS FRITH COLLECTION

www.francisfrith.com

ST NEOTS

A HISTORY & CELEBRATION

DAVID BUSHBY

THE FRANCIS FRITH COLLECTION

www.francisfrith.com

First published in the United Kingdom in 2005
by The Francis Frith Collection®

Hardback Edition 2005 ISBN 1-84589-216-X
Paperback Edition 2011 ISBN 978-1-84589-600-3

British Library Cataloguing in Publication Data

St Neots - A History & Celebration
David Bushby

The Francis Frith Collection
Oakley Business Park, Wylye Road,
Dinton, Wiltshire SP3 5EU
Tel: +44 (0) 1722 716 376
Email: info@francisfrith.co.uk
www.francisfrith.com

Printed and bound in England

Front Cover: **ST NEOTS, MARKET SQUARE c1965** S37044t

Additional modern photographs by David Bushby.

Domesday extract used in timeline by kind permission of
Alecto Historical Editions, www.domesdaybook.org
Aerial photographs reproduced under licence from
Simmons Aerofilms Limited.
Historical Ordnance Survey maps reproduced under licence from
Homecheck.co.uk

Every attempt has been made to contact copyright holders of
illustrative material. We will be happy to give full acknowledgement in
future editions for any items not credited. Any information should be
directed to The Francis Frith Collection.

*The colour-tinting in this book is for illustrative purposes only,
and is not intended to be historically accurate*

AS WITH ANY HISTORICAL DATABASE, THE FRANCIS FRITH ARCHIVE
IS CONSTANTLY BEING CORRECTED AND IMPROVED, AND THE
PUBLISHERS WOULD WELCOME INFORMATION ON OMISSIONS OR
INACCURACIES

CONTENTS

A HISTORY & CELEBRATION

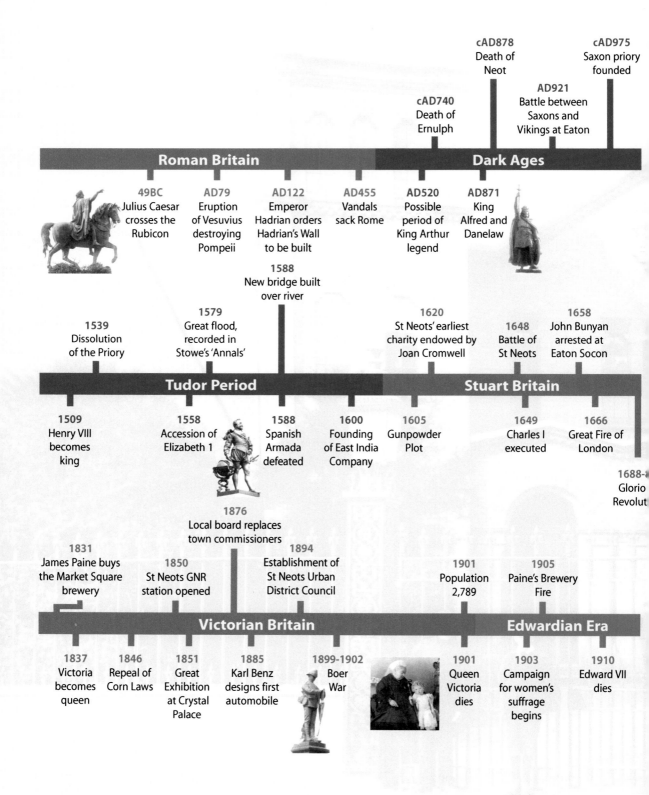

cAD878
Death of
Neot

cAD975
Saxon priory
founded

AD921
Battle between
Saxons and
Vikings at Eaton

cAD740
Death of
Ernulph

Roman Britain

Dark Ages

49BC
Julius Caesar
crosses the
Rubicon

AD79
Eruption
of Vesuvius
destroying
Pompeii

AD122
Emperor
Hadrian orders
Hadrian's Wall
to be built

AD455
Vandals
sack Rome

AD520
Possible
period of
King Arthur
legend

AD871
King
Alfred and
Danelaw

1588
New bridge built
over river

1579
Great flood,
recorded in
Stowe's 'Annals'

1620
St Neots' earliest
charity endowed by
Joan Cromwell

1648
Battle of
St Neots

1658
John Bunyan
arrested at
Eaton Socon

1539
Dissolution
of the Priory

Tudor Period

Stuart Britain

1509
Henry VIII
becomes
king

1558
Accession of
Elizabeth 1

1588
Spanish
Armada
defeated

1600
Founding
of East India
Company

1605
Gunpowder
Plot

1649
Charles I
executed

1666
Great Fire of
London

1688-
Glorio
Revolut

1876
Local board replaces
town commissioners

1831
James Paine buys
the Market Square
brewery

1850
St Neots GNR
station opened

1894
Establishment of
St Neots Urban
District Council

1901
Population
2,789

1905
Paine's Brewery
Fire

Victorian Britain

Edwardian Era

1837
Victoria
becomes
queen

1846
Repeal of
Corn Laws

1851
Great
Exhibition
at Crystal
Palace

1885
Karl Benz
designs first
automobile

1899-1902
Boer
War

1901
Queen
Victoria
dies

1903
Campaign
for women's
suffrage
begins

1910
Edward VII
dies

HISTORICAL TIMELINE FOR ST NEOTS

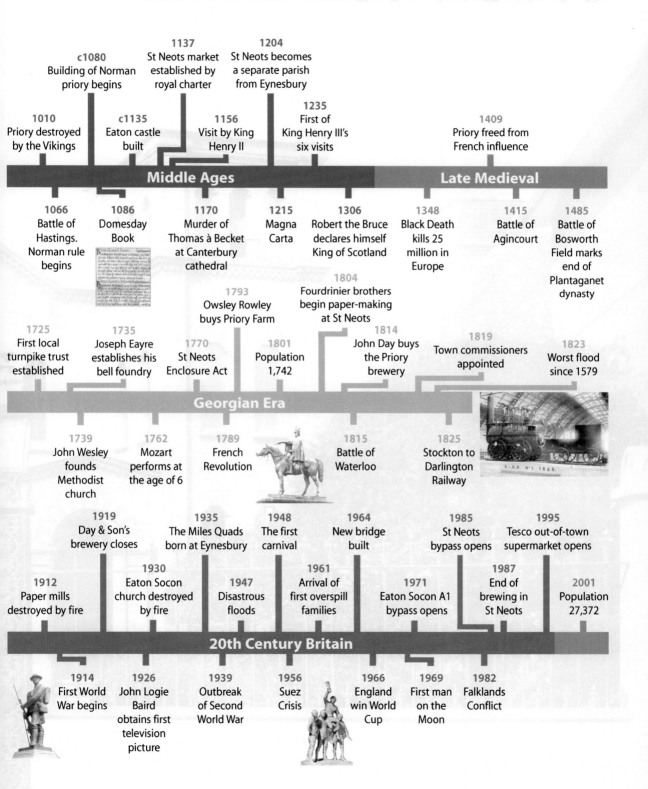

c1080
Building of Norman priory begins

1137
St Neots market established by royal charter

1204
St Neots becomes a separate parish from Eynesbury

1010
Priory destroyed by the Vikings

c1135
Eaton castle built

1156
Visit by King Henry II

1235
First of King Henry III's six visits

1409
Priory freed from French influence

Middle Ages

Late Medieval

1066
Battle of Hastings. Norman rule begins

1086
Domesday Book

1170
Murder of Thomas à Becket at Canterbury cathedral

1215
Magna Carta

1306
Robert the Bruce declares himself King of Scotland

1348
Black Death kills 25 million in Europe

1415
Battle of Agincourt

1485
Battle of Bosworth Field marks end of Plantaganet dynasty

1725
First local turnpike trust established

1735
Joseph Eayre establishes his bell foundry

1793
Owsley Rowley buys Priory Farm

1804
Fourdrinier brothers begin paper-making at St Neots

1770
St Neots Enclosure Act

1801
Population 1,742

1814
John Day buys the Priory brewery

1819
Town commissioners appointed

1823
Worst flood since 1579

Georgian Era

1739
John Wesley founds Methodist church

1762
Mozart performs at the age of 6

1789
French Revolution

1815
Battle of Waterloo

1825
Stockton to Darlington Railway

1919
Day & Son's brewery closes

1935
The Miles Quads born at Eynesbury

1948
The first carnival

1964
New bridge built

1985
St Neots bypass opens

1995
Tesco out-of-town supermarket opens

1912
Paper mills destroyed by fire

1930
Eaton Socon church destroyed by fire

1947
Disastrous floods

1961
Arrival of first overspill families

1971
Eaton Socon A1 bypass opens

1987
End of brewing in St Neots

2001
Population 27,372

20th Century Britain

1914
First World War begins

1926
John Logie Baird obtains first television picture

1939
Outbreak of Second World War

1956
Suez Crisis

1966
England win World Cup

1969
First man on the Moon

1982
Falklands Conflict

OUTSIDE its immediate neighbourhood St Neots seems to be virtually unknown. In 1997 one new road atlas even missed it off the map altogether! The town's main claim to fame, perhaps only remembered now outside the area by those of an older generation, is that it was the place where the first live birth of quads took place in the 1930s. Yet it is a town that not only has a wealth of history but that also seems set for an exciting future.

For centuries St Neots was a part of Huntingdonshire, but a two-county merger on 1 April 1974 took it into Cambridgeshire. In the last few decades it has grown from a small market town into the largest town in Cambridgeshire, and further considerable expansion lies ahead. The modern town comprises St Neots itself, Eynesbury, and the most populous parts of the old parish of Eaton Socon. The link with Eynesbury is an ancient one, but that with Eaton Socon only occurred with boundary changes brought about in the 1960s. Before then Eaton Socon, a Bedfordshire parish on the other side of the River Ouse, had been totally separate from St Neots, the river having provided a natural boundary between the two places.

The amalgamation of the parishes, together with the influx of London overspill and the large-scale housing developments of the last 45 years, has created a town that would leave the people of earlier generations amazed. Yet, what they did contributed significantly to the overall pattern of the town that is still recognisable in today's St Neots. It is their story, as well as that of the present-day town, that this book explores, celebrating their achievements, which have contributed to St Neots becoming the busy, thriving place that it is today.

CHAPTER ONE

HAPPENINGS ALONG THE RIVER

THE RIVER c1965 S37068

This tranquil scene belies the violence that often occurred along the river in earlier times.

THE MAIN INFLUENCE on the early development of the area which today is St Neots was the River Ouse. Early settlers were attracted by its fertile banks and grew their crops there, despite the risk posed by frequent flooding. The Romans, too, grew corn locally to feed their legions, and no doubt transported some of it along the river. Regular finds of coins, pottery and other artefacts have given evidence of an established Roman community on both banks. There is evidence of a Roman villa at Eaton which had its own vineyard, and this still existed in the late 11th century, as it features in the Domesday survey of 1086. It was even remembered centuries later: one of

the field names at the time of the enclosure in the late 18th century was Vineyard Field. After the Romans left the Saxons occupied the area, again on both sides of the river, and it was during this period that settlements at Eynesbury and Eaton emerged. St Neots eventually developed within Eynesbury parish, on the site of the present town centre. Eynesbury derives its name from an individual called Ainulph or Ernulph. One legend claims that he was of the royal line of the ancient Britons, but probably he was simply a holy man who lived here as a hermit. After his death, in or around AD 740, he came to be venerated by the Saxons of the area and it is possible that the first religious building in the area was one associated with, or dedicated to, Ainulph. The region of the Saxon settlement was off the present Church Street and Cambridge Street, and along the brook now known as Hen Brook, later to become the boundary between Eynesbury and St Neots. Their burial ground was to the north of this, in the part of the town now occupied by Avenue Road. This Saxon cemetery was discovered when the town's expansion eastwards began in 1886. Several skeletons and various artefacts were unearthed. Unfortunately, there was little awareness of the archaeological significance of the finds, and what could have provided important details of the area during Saxon times was lost under the bricks and mortar of Victorian development.

It was almost certainly the Romans who provided us with the area's earliest legend. This tells of how there was a giant at Eynesbury Coneygeare at the river's edge who used to throw missiles at another giant situated on the Hillings mound at Eaton Socon, across the other side of the river. Like similar giant legends in other parts of the country, this probably grew up among people who only vaguely remembered the Romans and their works; and would have originated from memories of their large, stone-throwing catapults.

EYNESBURY CONEYGEARE 2005 S37701k (David Bushby)

Eynesbury Coneygeare, the alleged lair of a giant and a former Roman station, is today a recreation area.

AVENUE ROAD 2005 S37702k (David Bushby)

Avenue Road, the site of the Saxon cemetery.

In the later Saxon period the history of the locality was shaped both by events along the river, and also by the circumstances surrounding the establishment of the priory from which the town of St Neots was to develop. The area lay uncomfortably near the boundary of the Saxon and Viking regions of influence, and early in the 10th century the Vikings moved their forces along the River Ouse towards Bedford, creating fortifications along the way. A major fortification was the earthworks now known as the Hillings at Eaton Socon. In AD 921 the Viking advance was checked at Bedford and they were driven back. It seems that the Eaton earthworks were besieged, and taken after fierce fighting.

Those killed in the conflict were buried on the Hillings site. An excavation in 1949 found 40 bodies in one trench, some of which had clearly died a violent death. An earlier excavation claimed to have uncovered swords and the bodies of warriors, but this has never been verified.

It is thought that a stone church was built at the Hillings to celebrate the Saxon victory, and that the settlement of Eaton grew up around it. 'Ton' is a common place-name ending in this area, referring to a farming settlement. The first part of the name, the Ea- component, relates to the river, so giving us the meaning 'river farmstead'. The 'Socon' part of the name does not appear until the 13th century when Eaton achieved the status of a soke (a place that had the right of local jurisdiction), giving it freedom from the local hundred court of Barford.

Meanwhile, on the other side of the river during the late Saxon period, what was to become St Neots was emerging as a distinct development within Eynesbury parish. It was in or around AD 975 that a Saxon nobleman whose name was probably Leofric, and his wife Leofleda, established a priory at Eynesbury. Its location is not known, although it is unlikely to have been on the riverside site occupied by the later Norman priory. Most probably it was near the Saxon settlement, and there is evidence to suggest that it was on the site of the present parish church. The important point for the town's development is that Leofric's desire to give his priory status and make it a centre of veneration led to the acquisition from Cornwall of the bones of St Neot.

Little is known for certain about Neot except that he became a monk at Glastonbury Abbey, where he established a reputation as an outstanding teacher. After a while he left the abbey and became a hermit on the edge of Bodmin Moor near the village of Hamstoke (sometimes referred to as Guerris-stoke, and now called St Neot). Later (following, it is said, a visit to the Pope) he founded a small monastery there. One strand of his story tells how King Alfred the Great visited him at Hamstoke. Neot was supposed to have had a considerable influence on him, helping him in his battles against the Vikings. When Neot died, possibly in the year AD 878 and traditionally on 31 July (this date was to become his feast day), he was buried in the monastery church. Stories soon started to circulate of miraculous cures that had occurred at his tomb and Neot was in due course canonised.

THE ALFRED JEWEL

In 1693 a small object, oval in shape and made of gold, was found near the site of Athelney Abbey in Somerset. On the front is the figure of a man holding two staffs. Round its edge are the words 'Aelfred mec heht gewyrcan' (Alfred had me made). It is known as the Alfred Jewel and is now in the Ashmolean Museum in Oxford. One conjecture is that the figure is meant to represent St Neot. Although this idea has been largely discredited, the jewel is still very much regarded as a symbol of St Neots, appearing on St Neots crested china, the former Urban District Council's headed stationery and its chairman's chain of office, as well as more recently in the form of a mosaic in the Market Square.

THE GOSS URN 2005 ZZZ04672 (David Bushby)

The Goss urn, showing the Alfred Jewel crest.

Why Leofric wanted the bones of St Neot for his priory, or even how he had heard of this relatively obscure Cornish saint, we shall never know. What seems certain is that to get them from Cornwall to Huntingdonshire deception and possibly theft were employed, apparently with the authorisation of King Edgar and several prominent churchmen. The arrangements for the transfer of the bones to their new home were left to the warden of St Neot's shrine. The story goes that he set off with them from Cornwall on 30 November AD 975 in inclement wintry weather, and arrived in Eynesbury on 7 December. Meanwhile the Cornish villagers, alarmed by the disappearance of the warden, examined the shrine and found to their dismay that the bones of their saint had gone. They armed themselves, and having first searched the immediate neighbourhood, followed the warden to Eynesbury, threatening all manner of violence if their saint was not returned. According to one story King Edgar had to send troops to drive them back to Cornwall.

A chapel was erected to receive the saint's remains and many eminent churchmen attended the dedication ceremony. At Leofric's request monks were sent from Ely and Thorney to establish the new priory. It was arranged that it should become a daughter house of Ely, which meant that it became a Benedictine priory, with the prior appointed by the mother house. Further, Leofric provided for his priory's financial security by endowing it with 960 acres of land in Eynesbury, Gamlingay and Waresley.

This early prosperity of Leofric's priory was short-lived, as the Vikings soon renewed their attacks on the area. Fears for the safety of St Neot's remains led to them being sent to Crowland Abbey in Lincolnshire, as representing a safer place of refuge. Such a precaution proved to have been a wise one, as the priory was in all probability devastated by Viking marauders in 1010. They had sailed along the Ouse from Buckinghamshire as far as Tempsford, where they left their boats and marched to Ipswich, burning and pillaging as they went.

Some believe that not only was the priory destroyed, but that it remained in a desolate condition. The evidence, though, indicates that it was restored, in part if not totally, and the bones of St Neot were returned from Crowland - although not without difficulty. It was not unusual for religious houses to try to hold on to relics entrusted to them in times of danger, and that certainly happened in this case. Indeed, Crowland claimed that the bones never were returned and for many years afterwards maintained that they were still there at the abbey. However, in 1078-79 Anselm, later to become Archbishop of Canterbury but then the newly-appointed Abbot of Bec, visited Neotsbury, as the town had then generally come to be called, and inspected the bones. He was convinced that they were indeed the bones of St Neot. Also it would appear that he took a jawbone back with him to Bec, and so the bones of St Neot became even more scattered.

After the Viking incursions of the early 11th century there was a more settled period during which the area prospered. By 1066 there were several settlements and evidence of what was, by the standards of the time, a considerable population. Eaton was the most diverse of the parishes, with various hamlets covering a considerable 7,600 acres, making it the largest parish in Bedfordshire. What was to become Eaton village comprised just less than 2,500 acres of arable land, with enough meadow land to sustain the teams of oxen needed to work such an area. There was woodland sufficient for 400 pigs, two mills, an ample supply of eels from the river, as well as the small vineyard already referred to. Thane Wulfmer of Eaton, Bedfordshire's second largest landowner, must have found it a very pleasant place in which to have lived.

Eynesbury had developed as a village of similar proportions to Eaton, and had its own church and priest. The Domesday book tells us that it was a royal manor, belonging to Edward the Confessor, and had substantial arable land, meadow and sixty acres of woodland pasture. There was also sufficient fold for more than 600 sheep - a particularly interesting entry, as it forms the only reference to sheep in the whole of the Domesday survey of Huntingdonshire.

Fact File

One curious footnote to the story is that the Cornish St Neot was not left entirely without its saint. An inventory of the locations of saints' bones, made in the 11th century, claimed that St Neot was at St Neots in Huntingdonshire but that one arm was still at St Neot in Cornwall!

Along with its two mills, there is evidence of another flourishing village.

St Neots, still officially a part of Eynesbury at the time of Domesday, was even more flourishing. Eynesbury's value in 1066 was put at £20, but that of St Neots was given as £24. Robert, son of Wymare held 1,800 acres of arable land there, and, along with the inevitable mill, there was also a fishery. All in all, the scene in the St Neots area on the eve of the Norman Conquest was one of order and prosperity.

EATON SOCON, THE MILL AND GREAT OUSE c1960 E202019

There was a working mill on the Ouse at Eaton Socon from Saxon times until the 20th century. Today it is the River Mill bar and restaurant.

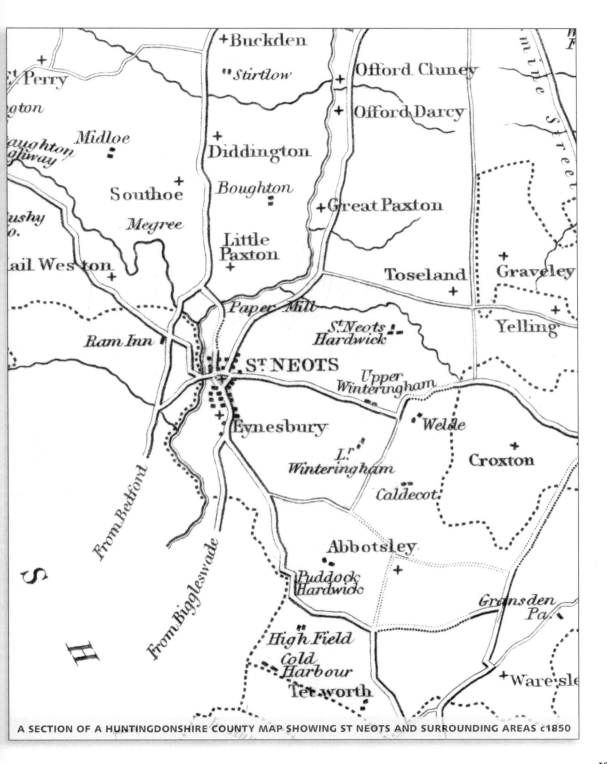

A SECTION OF A HUNTINGDONSHIRE COUNTY MAP SHOWING ST NEOTS AND SURROUNDING AREAS c1850

MARKET PLACE 1925 77214a

CHAPTER TWO

THE RISE AND FALL OF ST NEOTS PRIORY AND THE GROWTH OF A MARKET TOWN

AS THE all-conquering Norman army moved up into England, it passed through this area, crossing the Ouse just south of St Neots at Little Barford, and possibly also at Eaton Ford. Two of the three manors changed hands as the old Saxon order was largely swept away. Eaton was first granted to one of William's soldiers, Lisois de Moutiers, but it soon passed from him to Eudo, the King's steward, and eventually, in or just after 1120, to a junior branch of the de Beauchamp family. The senior branch of this family already held Bedford, and the junior branch set about establishing itself firmly as barons of Eaton. Some time after 1135, during the increasingly violent struggle for the throne between Stephen and Matilda, Hugh de Beauchamp demolished the original church on the raised Hillings site and built a castle there to defend his position. This was a hastily erected wooden castle, not the stone structure of popular imagination, and it seems likely that it was never even fully completed. It was almost certainly one of the many illegal castles that sprang up at that time, and it was demolished once the country had settled down again under Henry II. As a result of these upheavals a new church had to be built, and this was erected on the site of the present building. This in turn helped to change the focus of the village, which was to develop along the Great North Road, as it is today. In about 1195 Eaton also gained its own religious house with the establishment of Bushmead Priory on the

THE HILLINGS MOUND ZZZ04673 (Norris Museum)

The Hillings Mound with Eaton Socon church in the background, from a 19th-century drawing.

edge of the parish, but this never gained the significance of its St Neots neighbour. It is clear though that in this and other ways the de Beauchamps of Eaton did try to rival the success of St Neots, of which they may have been jealous, or even suspicious.

Eynesbury initially provided some continuity after 1066, as Earl Waltheof, who had held the manor for the king before the Conquest, was allowed to retain his lands as he had married Judith, the Conqueror's niece. Unfortunately he became involved in a rebellion against William and was executed; so by 1086 Eynesbury was held by the Countess Judith alone.

The most interesting developments at Eynesbury during the 12th century were the building of a stone church on the site of today's church, and the creation of a rabbit warren on the site of the old Roman fortifications down towards the river. There was a church at Eynesbury, dedicated to St Mary, at the time of Domesday but no part of this has survived. The present Eynesbury church is a hotchpotch of various architectural styles, but the earliest remaining parts have been dated back to the later 12th century. As the village of Eynesbury developed it was in a triangle out from the church, and this basic pattern can still be seen, along Berkley Street, Luke Street and Montagu Street. There was also development, inevitably, along the road leading into St Neots itself, now called St Mary's Street.

EYNESBURY, ST MARY'S STREET c1965 E216050

THE RABBIT WARREN

The rabbit warren, a symbol of the status and prestige of the local lords of the manor, can be traced back to a reference in 1279 but was probably established much earlier. The rabbit was brought to England by the Normans and was a luxury, highly prized both for its meat and its fur. It was not the hardy creature of today and did not adapt easily to the English winters. Because of this, as well as its value, it was kept in specially constructed warrens, enclosed against predators and with a warrener in charge. The mound near the river, possibly created originally by the Romans, was no doubt ideal for this purpose. In later times the site was excavated for gravel and is now completely flat. Its past use is still remembered in its name, the Coneygeare, which simply means rabbit warren.

The most significant developments after 1066 occurred at St Neots, where the priory was reconstituted and rebuilt, and became a focal point for pilgrims and visitors. The manor here passed to the powerful de Clare family in the person of Earl Gilbert de Clare, a man totally opposed to the original priory's mother house, Ely Abbey, which had resisted William's accession to the English throne. It is thought that de Clare tricked the monks at St Neots Priory, who were themselves unhappy with the extent of Ely's power over them. By whatever means he did it, he managed to gain control of the priory, and in 1078 handed it over to the great Abbey of Bec in France, expelling the unfortunate English monks. This made St Neots what was known as an alien cell, and later led to its sequestration on the various occasions when there was war between England and France. On the positive side, it was occupied by eighteen monks

from Bec, a place in the mainstream of the European culture of its day. This helped to make St Neots a centre of learning, as well as attracting people to the town because of the shrine of St Neot.

Richard de Clare, son of Gilbert, had married Rohais, daughter of Eudo, who at that point held the manor of Eaton. In about 1080 they decided to rebuild the priory on more substantial lines than before, a task that seems to have taken many years. Sadly, nothing of these Norman buildings remains visible today, but excavations have shown both their extent, covering at least 50 acres, and their effect on the pattern of the town as it is today. The line of buildings along the north side of the Market Square marks the front boundary, and the site then stretches back almost to St Neots Common. The various excavations have uncovered foundations of some of the priory buildings, including what is believed to have been its church. The truth remains, however, that we still have only a limited idea of what St Neots Priory was like.

The new priory soon began to attract rich endowments, beginning with Rohais, now a widow, who became regarded as its second founder. In 1113 she 'gave to God and to St Mary of Bec and St Neot and to the monks of Eynesbury the manor of Eynesbury and all its appurtenances which she then held'. Further gifts, great and small, also followed, including other lands and fisheries, as well as money. Often the gifts of money were in some way or other intended for the use of the priory church, especially for lights to burn before the feretory that contained the bones of St Neot.

> ## Fact File
>
> *A feretory was a portable shrine. This would probably have been carried in procession through the town on such days as the feast of St Neot on 31 July and the festival of St Neot on 7 December. The festival marked the day when his bones were said to have arrived from Cornwall.*

Important among other gifts to the priory were the advowsons of a number of churches, among them that of Eynesbury church. This advowson was granted on condition that, as the priory was close to the great 'thoroughfare and celebrated road' from

MARKET SQUARE c1955 S37021

This row of buildings on the north side of the Market Square marks the front boundary of the priory.

London to York, the prior and monks should 'give meat and drink, for the love of God, to all who should ask them'. Such hospitality was, of course, a major function of religious houses during the medieval period. The route of the Great North Road, passing near the one and through the other, indicates one of the reasons why St Neots and Eaton were important to travellers. They were to remain so for many centuries; while Eynesbury village, not being on a major road, was much more of a backwater.

As travellers and pilgrims increased, so the area around the priory developed as a trading place. A market area was established on the site of the present Market Square, which claims to be among the largest in the country. There were temporary booths, the remains of one of which were found during excavations in 1954. Later more permanent

MARKET SQUARE c1955 S37002

shops were erected.

The market was established by royal charter in about 1137. The monks were also granted the right to hold three fairs during the year. A later charter increased this to four. These fairs continued to be held for many centuries and one, the Holy Thursday (Ascension Day) Fair, continued to be known by that name until recent times, when it simply became the May Fair. All this contributed to the development of the town, which grew along the present High Street up to the town cross, which was situated at the junction of the St Neots-Cambridge and Eynesbury-Godmanchester roads, a point still known as the Cross today. It is claimed that the position of the cross went back to the arrival of the bones of St Neot in the area, according to tradition marking their original resting place.

HUNTINGDON STREET c1955 S37004

The junction of Church Street, High Street, Huntingdon Street and Cambridge Street, believed to be the site of the medieval town cross.

For many years there had been no bridge over the Ouse for people to cross from Eaton to St Neots, and travellers and visitors had needed to rely on the ford or a ferry. The new development and prestige of the priory, and the growth of the town around it, made a bridge necessary, and one was built during the middle part of the 12th century, certainly by 1180. It was a long, narrow, wooden structure, and, one suspects, none too safe! This is illustrated by an accident in 1254, when the Earl of Derby, suffering from gout, was being carried across it on a stretcher. His servants managed to tip him off, over the bridge, and on to the ground at the edge of

the river. He later died of his injuries. The priory was responsible for the maintenance of the bridge right up until the Dissolution and could charge a toll for people using it.

The accident to the Earl of Derby highlights the fact that important people did come to visit the shrine of St Neot. In the 12th and 13th centuries this even extended to royalty: King Henry II making a visit there in 1156. It must have become a favourite place for King Henry III, as no less than six visits are recorded between 23 March 1235 and 23-24 August 1249. Normal court business was transacted on these occasions, so he would, no doubt, have brought a large retinue with him and much hospitality would have been required, again indicating how St Neots must have grown. The king was praised by the monks because he attended mass three times a day.

ST NEOTS SEAL ZZZ04674

The seal of St Neots Priory, depicting the Virgin and Child with Neot kneeling (from G C Gorham's History of St Neots, 1820).

The priory attracted important visitors, and there were also burials of prominent people within the priory church. Traditionally, these included the warden of the shrine of St Neot, who had brought his bones to the town. While

that is perhaps only a legend, it is certain that an extensive burial ground existed. It was situated just behind the frontage of shops on the north side of the Market Square, as all excavations there for extensions and new developments have revealed burials dating from the medieval period onwards.

St Neots had officially remained part of Eynesbury parish during its 12th-century period of development, but had obviously outgrown its more humble neighbour. Steps were taken in the late 12th century to establish St Neots as a separate parish, and this eventually happened in 1204. It would have been following this that the first parish church, as distinct from the priory church, was built for the town. We do not have an exact date for this, but in 1218 there is reference to Walter, chaplain of the parish church. Little of this original church remains, although parts were incorporated into later 14th- and 15th-century rebuildings.

As well as marking the ecclesiastical separation of St Neots from Eynesbury, the building of the parish church was also an indication of a growing urban independence and prosperity. Eaton and Eynesbury also flourished during this period, although they remained entirely rural, under the control of their various manors. The main interest of these years was in changes in the ownership of land. There are indications, especially at Eaton Socon, that there were moves to extend the amount of land under cultivation, with a number of references to assarted land - that is land that had been cleared of scrub or trees so that it might become arable land.

A sign of the growth of Eynesbury is the way in which the church was extended in the middle of the 13th century, with the rebuilding of the chancel and the addition of a south aisle and arcade, as well as a spire. This latter was to prove something of a liability in the long term, as it was eventually to collapse. Such a collapse also affected the priory church, as the bell tower there fell down in 1265, and in this disaster some of the most important of its charters were destroyed.

This was not, though, the worst setback to the priory's prosperity. The fact that it was an alien cell, linked to Bec in France, meant that every time there was conflict between England and France it was confiscated by the Crown, and was expected to contribute substantially to the royal exchequer. This happened in 1245, 1285, 1337 and 1370. On one occasion the monks, suspected of subversive activities, were even forced out of their priory for a while, although eventually they were allowed to return. These events meant that that there were fewer visitors to the shrine of St Neot, and consequently less income all round. This is perhaps one reason why by the middle of the 14th century the bridge across the Ouse had fallen into a ruinous state.

The 14th century also saw the Black Death sweep across the area with devastating effect, much as it did elsewhere. There is, unfortunately, no clear record of how many died locally, but the small manor of Sudbury in Eaton Ford disappeared altogether, its demise possibly a result of the plague. Two chantry priests at Eaton died, as did the Prior of Bushmead. The number of ordinary people who succumbed must have been considerable as a reference in the priory's cartulary for 1350 speaks of the scarcity of servants owing to the plague. Even towards the end of the century the priory was struggling, and its finances were clearly depleted as the monks were not able to afford repairs to three of their mills that had been damaged by floods. This is an early indication that the floods which were to cause so many problems for St Neots in the 19th and 20th centuries were nothing new.

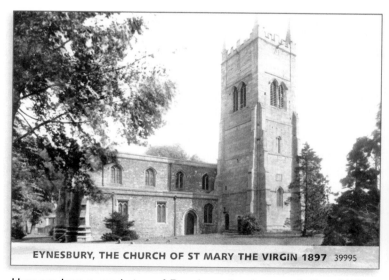

EYNESBURY, THE CHURCH OF ST MARY THE VIRGIN 1897 39995

Here we have a good view of Eynesbury church tower, built in 1687 to replace the spire, which had collapsed two years earlier after being struck by lightning.

30

The 1300s also saw the rise of local guilds, the first being formed at Eaton Socon in about 1343. This was the Guild of Corpus Christi which, like similar guilds nationwide, had both a religious and a social purpose. It employed a priest to say masses for members at the guild altar in Eaton church, and also had a guild hall where members met to eat together. Here, on the Sunday after Corpus Christi, the members would gather to elect two of their number to serve as masters for the ensuing year. There was also a Guild of Jesus formed at St Neots, although the date of its foundation is not known. The earliest recorded gift to it is 1516, but the guild probably existed long before then. It was run on similar lines to its Eaton counterpart, including women as well as men among its members. It clearly became quite prosperous and built, as part of the parish church, the Jesus Chapel (which still exists) for its own altar.

The early 15th century was particularly important to St Neots Priory. The French influence had been declining for some time - three French monks had returned home to France in 1378, leaving only four, including the prior. When he died in 1404 an Englishman was elected to replace him and five years later all ties with Bec were severed, which meant that St Neots was now a totally English priory. This was not an immediate recipe for prosperity - far from it - and in the 1430s the priory buildings were in a desperate state, needing extensive repair. The church roof leaked and there was no longer a guest hall. The monks themselves were slack in following their rule and were at

odds with the sub-prior and the prior, who was suspected of an improper relationship with a married woman. As the century progressed, however, the structural defects were remedied and the discipline improved; and the priory returned to something like its former prosperity.

This renewed prosperity is reflected also in the rebuilding of the churches at Eaton Socon and St Neots. At Eaton Socon in about 1430 a fine tower was built, the nave was lengthened and made loftier by the addition of a clerestory, and a new chancel was also constructed. Perhaps the most glorious feature of the new church was its stained glass, filling every window, with stories of the saints on the north side, and scenes from the New Testament on the south.

The work at St Neots was equally dramatic and produced the splendid church that still stands today. It is, beyond doubt, the finest building in the area and is sometimes referred to as the Cathedral of Huntingdonshire. It reflects both the wealth that there must have been in the town at that time and the devotion of the people. Building work began around 1485 and lasted for about nine years. Money was left for making the rood in 1486, an important feature in the devotions of the time. The greatest splendour of the new church, however, was its imposing tower, rising up as it does some 128 feet to its pinnacles.

Compared with what happened at Eaton and St Neots, work at Eynesbury was on a much more modest scale. Nonetheless a clerestory was added here also, giving a

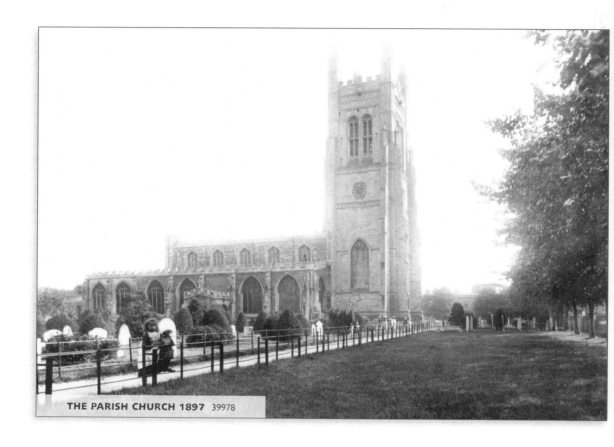

THE PARISH CHURCH 1897 39978

greater sense of height and light. Some of the benches that are still in the church date from this period. They have ornate carved ends, some in the shape of birds or exotic animals, and these have led to them becoming known locally as the Eynesbury Zoo.

Other significant changes were also taking place. In the rural economy there was less arable farming and an increased emphasis on sheep farming, which required a smaller labour force. This led to the creation of large common areas near to the town which are still in evidence today.

As there was a growth in wealth in this period, so more substantial dwellings were erected, and limited signs of these can be found in present-day St Neots. The best example is on the High Street, and is now Freeman's jeweller's shop. St Neots has, however, suffered badly in comparison with other Huntingdonshire towns, and this building survived more by chance than design. At some point the original timber frame had been clad in brick, and it was, in fact, bought by Alfred Freeman in 1955 with a view to its being demolished. However, when the original construction was uncovered, it was, fortunately, decided to restore it to what in had been. Its original occupant would probably have been a well-to-do merchant.

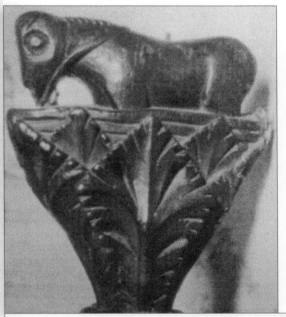 

TWO CREATURES FROM THE 'ZOO' IN EYNESBURY CHURCH ZZZ04675 (Norris Museum)

During the early 16th century both priory and town prospered; and many visitors again came to the shrine of St Neot. Others came to buy and sell in the market or at the various fairs. One notable visitor who visited the town in 1538 was John Leland, library-keeper and antiquary to Henry VIII. His purpose was to examine the relics held by the priory as part of a scheme to seek out and list the antiquities of the kingdom. It is said that he was shown a hair-cloth vest, reputedly worn by St Neot, and a comb supposedly used by him.

By the time of Leland's visit dramatic and wide-sweeping changes were taking place which would lead to the seemingly settled world of town and priory being torn apart as a result of the marriage problems of Henry VIII and his resulting conflict with the papacy. Within a few years the guilds of Jesus and of Corpus Christi, Bushmead Priory, and, most of all, St Neots Priory, had all been swept away and their considerable lands and properties confiscated to the state. There was nothing that anyone locally could do about this, although it seems that there was some resistance from the monks of St Neots Priory and also an attempt to hide the assets of the Jesus Guild from the royal predators, but both gestures were in the end futile.

The old order was swept away and with it the relics of St Neot. What happened to the shrine, the bones, the shirt, or the comb is unknown, and none of them has ever been traced. The last prior, John Rawnds, who had resigned the priory to the King in 1539, and some other priests and monks in the area were

HIGH STREET 1925 77204

The building on the immediate left, clad in brick, was for many years the school house for the master of the boys' school in Church Walk.

pensioned off, while others were left to fend for themselves as best they could. St Neots Priory and its immediate lands were acquired by Sir Richard Williams of Hinchingbrooke in 1542.

HIGH STREET 2005 S37703k (David Bushby)

The same building today, restored to its original splendour

At that time it was reported that the bridge was in poor condition and in danger of falling down. The bill for its repair indicated that it was still a wooden construction. The old priory buildings were simply abandoned and allowed to decay. As happened in so many other places, the stones were taken away and used for buildings elsewhere. In 1588 a new timber and stone bridge was built across the river to replace the old one, and local tradition asserts that priory stone was used in the construction. This may have been so, but the bridge was subsequently reconstructed entirely of stone in the 17th century and was widened, repaired and altered on several later occasions, so that by 1964, when it was demolished, it is questionable as to how much of the original stone would have remained. So much stone was removed from the priory site in the years following the Dissolution that eventually only the gatehouse was left, and even that was demolished in 1814.

The townspeople of the second half of the 16th century found themselves worse off in various ways, especially as the son of Sir Richard Williams, who succeeded him to the priory lands, appropriated some of the former commons for his own exclusive use. The townspeople took the situation to arbitration, but lost out, barely managing to retain some of their commons and certain rights, such as keeping a common bull for breeding. As well as material deprivations, like this loss of common land, there was a spiritual loss. The churches, which no longer had the support of the local priories and chantry and guild

priests, were less well-equipped to minister to needs that had traditionally been met by the various religious institutions.

A further blow was that the church buildings themselves did not escape attack. As part of the ongoing Protestant Reformation, which was to gather pace during the short reign of Edward VI, commisioners were sent to the town in 1547 to pull down 'the images of abuse' in St Neots Church. They met with considerable opposition from the townspeople, whose leaders ordered them to put the images back again. When they refused they were threatened, and the situation became ugly. After several complaints by the commissioners, the ringleaders were summoned before the King's Council at Hampton Court and ordered to desist from such behaviour or face severe punishment. So the images had to go, but this was not

THE BRIDGE 1897 39983

final. The reign of Mary I, who restored Catholicism, brought another commission to the town, and this ordered that they should be reinstated by Easter 1557, at the expense, of course, of the unfortunate townspeople. This reversal of the situation was again only temporary and in August 1559, following the restoration of the Protestant faith under Queen Elizabeth I, commissioners finally demolished them.

Some things were saved from all the dramatic changes that had occurred. The educational work of the priory was able to continue in a school known as St Neots Grammar School. This was located in the Jesus Chapel of the parish church, vacated by the dissolution of the Guild. Several notable scholars were educated at it, and it seems to have continued for at least a hundred years, as there is reference to the schoolmaster receiving a payment of £20 in 1658. Whether it was still a grammar school then is not clear, however, and it would seem that it did eventually decline to become simply an elementary school, giving instruction in the basic 3Rs instead of in the classics as it had once done.

Another development, brought about indirectly by the changes of these years and the end of institutions such as St Neots Priory, was the rise in charitable benefactions. In earlier times pious people had left goods, lands and money to the priories and other religious institutions; so their end left a vacuum which came to be filled by charitable endowments to found or run schools or to support the poor. Eynesbury and Eaton did only moderately here, but St Neots itself became rich in charities, although the earliest recorded of these, Cromwell's Charity, only dates from 1620, much later than in many towns.

Changes in the church were matched by changes in the outside world, as the old social order was being broken down. Some successful tradesmen were becoming

THE PARISH REGISTERS

One of the most important features of the Tudor era was the beginning of parish registers, recording baptisms, marriages and burials. Of particular interest from the 16th century entries are those which show the influence of the Great North Road, bringing many travellers, a lot of them probably quite unwelcome. Some of them died locally and were buried unnamed and unknown. In March 1583 'an unknown girl' was buried at Eaton Socon, followed a few years later by 'two beggars, the one a widow, the other a boy'. In the next century a 'solger' suffered the same fate. Beggars and travellers, too, took their children to church for baptism. The number of references suggests that there was much more movement by poorer people in this period than is sometimes realised.

decidedly upwardly mobile. No longer was the local lord of the manor necessarily a nobleman, although the Earls of Sandwich were to acquire both St Neots and Eynesbury and hold them for many years. At Eaton, however, the manor was sold to a local man, Gaius Squire, in 1624 and when his son sold it later in the century, it was to Henry Ashley of Eynesbury, whose father had been a tanner. The sale price was £8,000, which must have been the equivalent of several million pounds today, indicating that some people, certainly, were managing to generate considerable wealth.

Some of this new wealth came through the regeneration of river transport along the Ouse. The river had always remained important for its mills, but it had become unnavigable in the centuries following the Viking raids along it. It was reopened to navigation, however, during the early 17th century. A new sluice was built to enable shipping to go beyond St Neots, and right up to Bedford; with its a tributary, the Ivel, also eventually being opened up through to Biggleswade and Shefford. This brought about a boom in river trade, which added to the prosperity of St Neots.

All the properties on the south side of the Market Square, some of which originate from the 17th century, backed down to Hen Brook and had the facility for goods to be brought in by boat. In fact, much of the lower part of this brook was important in the river trade and, if you stand on Eynesbury Bridge and look towards the main river, you can still see buildings whose original use was linked to it. It also helps to explain why several of the properties on Brook Street were public houses, catering for the needs of the boatmen who brought coal and other goods to the town.

THE BROOK c1955 S37012

BROOK STREET c1955 S37008

The building in the centre was formerly the White Swan public house.

A 17TH-CENTURY MYSTERY

On the side wall of the present Bridge House at the foot of St Neots Bridge is a 17th-century plaster panel with a curious design on it. This had been on the side of a butcher's shop which was once situated at the foot of the bridge, but when this shop was demolished in 1913, the panel was placed in its present position. Its origins have never been discovered, nor has its meaning - if it has one!

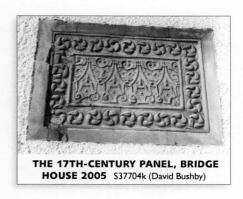

THE 17TH-CENTURY PANEL, BRIDGE HOUSE 2005 S37704k (David Bushby)

In the middle of the 17th century St Neots became involved in the conflict between King and Parliament. It might have been expected that local connections and influences would have produced a fairly solid support for the Parliamentary side, but this was by no means the case. The Earl of Sandwich was a Royalist, but his nephew, Sir Edward Montagu, sent troops to hold St Neots for Parliament in 1643. The Gerys of Bushmead were strong supporters of the Royalist cause, while Sir James Beverley, head of an important Eaton family, was a Parliamentarian. In 1645 the king passed through St Neots on his way to Woburn, gathering many recruits as he went, and these were sufficient to discourage any attack by Parliamentary forces.

St Neots did, however, see direct conflict during the Civil War, when a Royalist troop, having been defeated at Kingston on Thames, found its way to St Neots late one evening in July 1648. Early next morning they were attacked by a pursuing Parliamentary force under the command of Colonel Adrian Scroop. The bridge was stormed and the Royalists were overwhelmed in a short battle on the Market Square. Judged by most standards this would rate as little more than a skirmish, with twelve killed on the Royalist side and four on the Parliamentary, but its impact was considerable. The Royalists lost some important leaders, with Colonel Dolbier killed and the Earl of Holland captured, and the defeat was a severe blow to their morale. The event was celebrated in Parliament, a day of thanksgiving was proclaimed and a triumphalist pamphlet was published, all hailing it as a major victory.

The Civil War and Commonwealth period also had a considerable effect on the church, discouraging liturgy and ceremonial and enforcing a simpler and plainer religion. The aged Royalist vicar of Eaton Socon, Robert White, was expelled from his living. His successor, Thomas Becke, however, was almost

COLONEL SCROOP ZZZ04676 (Norris Museum)

Colonel Scroop, who led the Parliamentary troops at the battle of St Neots, was a signatory to the death warrant of Charles I and was executed in 1660.

equally a supporter of the old ways, and only survived through sheer determination in the face of considerable opposition. The fact that he did so suggests that, despite all the changes, the old ways remained strong in Eaton.

Church buildings again suffered during this period. It is said that most of the prisoners from the battle of St Neots were incarcerated in the parish church, and that Roundhead soldiers fired their muskets into the rafters as a mark of their disdain for the 'religious idolatry' in the building. Certainly some of the fine early stained glass windows were lost during this period. As elsewhere, the stone altar was replaced by a wooden communion table; but the vicar, Thomas Phage, seems to have held on to his living, despite the appointment of John Luke as Register of St Neots and Eynesbury in 1653. The restoration of the monarchy seven years later was no doubt greeted with considerable relief by the majority of local people, and there was much celebration and bell-ringing. For many years afterwards the local church bells were always rung to commemorate the anniversary of the king's return.

An insight into the size of the town and its satellite villages at this time is provided by the Hearth Tax returns of the 1670s. St Neots itself had 235 houses in 1674 and,

> ## Fact File
>
> *The New Inn on St Neots High Street is reputed to be haunted. There is a story that some of the prisoners were held there after the battle of St Neots and, since then, various people claim to have seen the cloaked form of a cavalier stalking the building.*

although 131 of these were the basic one-hearth dwellings, there were various larger houses, one even with fourteen and another with fifteen hearths. Eaton, a large, sprawling parish with various hamlets, had 202 houses, including several large ones. Eynesbury, on the other hand, had only 106 dwellings, most of which were small.

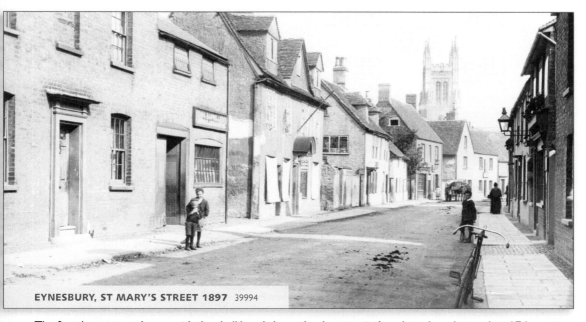

EYNESBURY, ST MARY'S STREET 1897 39994

The fine three-storey house with the shell hood above the doorway is thought to have been a late 17th-century farmhouse, and may have been one of the few large houses in Eynesbury at the time of the Hearth Tax.

A rising problem for all local authorities at this time was how to deal with the increasing number of poor people unable to support themselves. A late 17th-century return shows that St Neots was raising a rate for this purpose, and later all three parishes were to have their own workhouse.

One thing that the Commonwealth era had encouraged was the growth of nonconformity, but it was some time before it made any major impact locally. Eaton Socon was, though, one of the places where in 1658 the greatest dissenting writer and preacher

> ## Fact File
>
> *In 1983 a hoard of St Neots overseers' lace-making tokens was found in a 17th-century cottage that was being restored in St Mary's Street, Eynesbury.*

of his day, John Bunyan, had been arrested when he tried to preach there. It was in the outlying villages where Congregationalism took root, and it was from a church at Hail Weston that a meeting developed in

PILLOW LACE

One of the tasks given to girls and women in the workhouse was to make pillow lace. Legend says that this craft was introduced to the area by Catherine of Aragon, who was confined at nearby Buckden Towers and Kimbolton Castle following her divorce from Henry VIII, but this is unlikely. Lace-making was first recorded locally at Eaton Socon in 1586 when the overseers paid a woman 2d a week to teach poor children 'to worck bone lace'. This was made a condition for families wanting to claim poor relief, but later it became an important cottage industry at both Eynesbury and Eaton.

The importance locally of lace-making is illustrated by the tokens issued by St Neots overseers in the late 17th century, at a time when small change was scarce, which show two women engaged in this activity.

A DRAWING OF THE ST NEOTS OVERSEERS' TOKENS
ZZZ04677 (from G C Gorham's History of St Neots)

St Neots in 1701. A chapel, known as the Old Meeting, was erected in about 1717, and this survived into the 1960s, when sadly it was destroyed by fire. For most of the century this was the only nonconformist congregation in the town, and it was not until 1775 that a Methodist class was established: John Wesley making the first of a number of visits to St Neots. The Methodists obtained a building in Huntingdon Street, which they adapted as a chapel. A Baptist congregation was also established and a chapel was built in New Street in 1800.

There were other important developments in the area in the 18th century, not the least of which was the introduction and subsequent growth of stagecoach travel. Stagecoaches from London to the north began in 1706, but must have found the going difficult in the local area, as the Great North Road was in an appalling condition. In 1725, however, a turnpike trust was set up to put the section between Biggleswade

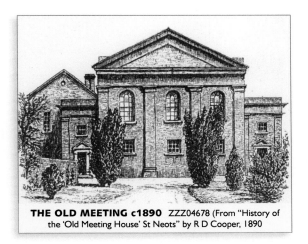

THE OLD MEETING c1890 ZZZ04678 (From "History of the 'Old Meeting House' St Neots" by R D Cooper, 1890

and Alconbury into good order, and both St Neots and Eaton benefited. In the heyday of the stagecoach it is said that more than 30 coaches daily either passed through Eaton village or took the loop through St Neots. The White Horse, Eaton Socon, and the Cross Keys, St Neots, were among the hostelries that prospered as coaching inns and supported a thriving industry, while the Cock at Eaton Socon, with its noted cuisine, catered for wealthier travellers.

EATON SOCON, THE WHITE HORSE AND GREAT NORTH ROAD c1960 E202012

A GRUESOME TALE

Of the local murders that have occurred over the years none is more gruesome than the one that happened in 1740. A townswoman had been to an outlying village to collect a legacy of £17. She decided to tie the coins up in her hair for safe-keeping. On her way home she met a neighbour, a butcher, and confided to him what she had done. He took the opportunity of a quiet spot to murder her and cut off her head, which he dropped into his bag. Unfortunately for him, a man and his servant were following close behind and came across the headless body. Catching up with the butcher, the servant engaged him in conversation, while his master rode ahead to alert the constable. At first he was incredulous but, on opening the butcher's bag, he found that the head was none other than that of his own wife! The butcher was duly arrested, tried and hanged.

Fact File

Samuel Pepys reputedly visited the White Horse and complained about the plainness of the maids! Charles Dickens must have known about the inn, although there is no record of him having visited it. In 'Nicholas Nickleby', Wackford Squeers and Nicholas stopped at the inn in Eaton Slocomb, as Dickens called it, on their stagecoach journey north to Dotheboys Hall!

During these years St Neots remained basically a market town, supporting an agricultural community, but other businesses did become important, in addition to those surrounding the inns and coaching. Brewing was, of course, closely related to both agriculture and inns. This area, partly, no doubt, owing to the coaching and other business brought by the Great North Road, had one of the highest proportions of inns and public and beer houses per head of the population of any town in England. It is no surprise that a thriving brewing industry developed! The major St Neots brewers of the 18th century occupied part of the Market Square and part of the old priory site along by the river. It is likely that the brewing on the priory site was simply a continuation of that which would have been carried on by the monks before the Dissolution, although William Fowler built new brewery buildings there in 1782. Of these the barley kiln is the only part that still stands today.

The most important new industry, however, was the bell-founding and clock-making business established in 1735 by Joseph Eayre on the other part of the old priory site. Here he is known to have cast over 40 bells for Huntingdonshire churches, and many more for other neighbouring counties. He also supplied various churches, including Eaton Socon, with

THE BARLEY KILN 2005 S37705k (David Bushby)

The Barley Kiln is now a part of the Riverside Snooker Club.

clocks. In addition, he made grandfather clocks, weighing machines, all sorts of metal items, and supplied fire engines, and was, not surprisingly perhaps, admired by his contemporaries for his versatility. On Eayre's death the business was taken over by a cousin, Edward Arnold, and then by Robert Taylor. He moved to Oxford in the early 1820s and bell-founding at St Neots came to an end. Members of the Taylor family later moved to Loughborough, and established the famous bell foundry which is still in operation today.

One important contribution that Joseph Eayre made to the town, which can still be seen today, is the building on the corner of High Street and Huntingdon Street. On the ground floor it was first a public house and later shops, but on the first floor were the Assembly Rooms. It was here that John Wesley, the founder of Methodism, preached on at least one occasion, and it

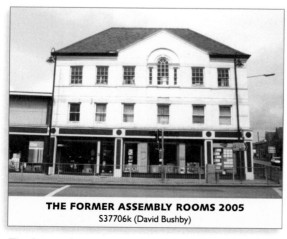

THE FORMER ASSEMBLY ROOMS 2005
S37706k (David Bushby)

The former Assembly Rooms, now part of the Westgate Co-op.

> ## Fact File
> Eynesbury Church still has a complete ring of six bells by Robert Taylor, which were cast in St Neots in 1810. They were restored and retuned in 2001.

also became the venue for a wide range of events as the social and cultural life of the town developed.

The 18th century also saw the establishment of continuous elementary education in the town. A major problem for schools in the days before state funding was that of providing the financial security which would ensure continuity. This happened in St Neots as a result of three charitable endowments between 1730 and 1760. The school, held for many years in the parish church, had a limited curriculum and was for boys only. Well into the 19th century the charity boys had to wear green jackets, leading to the nickname of the 'green linnets'.

St Neots had long been the centre for many surrounding farming communities, and had a number of farms within its own boundaries. It was affected by the important changes that were taking place during the 18th century which made the ancient style of open-field farming obsolete. These changes were to lead to the development of farms in their modern form, as St Neots (1770), Eynesbury (1795), and Eaton Socon (1797) were all enclosed by Acts of Parliament. Of the three Acts, that relating to St Neots is the

TWO GREEN LINNETS ZZZ04679 (Norris Museum)

Two 'Green Linnets' from a 19th-century watercolour.

most interesting. At Eaton and Eynesbury the common lands were enclosed along with the rest, but at St Neots the commons were retained, with 154 common rights being allocated. This number remains the same today, and meetings of the Common Proprietors are still held.

The enclosure of parishes led to important social change, helping on the one hand to promote the development of a thriving middle class with a number of well-to-do tenant farmers, but on the other creating a landless class dependent on employment as agricultural labourers.

A further significant event took place in 1793 when the Rowley family moved to St Neots. In that year Owsley Rowley bought Priory Farm, and then proceeded to build a large new house, Priory Hill House, at its highest point. He also created the spacious Priory Park around it. Over the years more land was added to the estate, and eventually the lordship of the manor of St Neots, which included the market rights, was purchased from the Earl of Sandwich. The patronage of St Neots Church was also acquired. This gave the Rowley family considerable influence in the town, an influence which is still felt today.

THE COMMON c1955 S37019

CHAPTER THREE

A CENTURY OF MAJOR SOCIAL AND ECONOMIC CHANGE

MARKET PLACE 1897 39974v

THE 19TH CENTURY brought only a slow population growth to St Neots with an increase that was well below the national average. In other ways, though, there were radical changes, especially as the transport revolution of the middle years of the century helped to broaden people's horizons. Many people, too, gained a greater sense of pride about being inhabitants of St Neots. Among the business and professional classes there developed a new social awareness and more time for leisure activities.

The early years of the century were not promising, however, as poverty became more widespread among the labouring classes. Lawlessness increased and St Neots became a hotbed of crime, despite efforts by the local Town Commissioners to curb it by the appointment of night-watchmen. A report in 1828 claimed: 'The inhabitants of St Neots continue to be much alarmed by the nightly depradations visited upon them.' Houses were broken into at night, while shops were often robbed in broad daylight. Sheep stealing and arson became alarmingly common as agricultural discontent escalated; and any individuals foolhardy enough to venture beyond the town boundaries after dark were in danger of attack by footpads. In December 1836 a further report stated: 'Sheep stealing and highway robbery have become very alarming ... in the neighbourhood of St Neots. We understand a London policeman is down, and has already taken several persons into custody.' Most of these crimes, it may be said, were those of unemployed and destitute men desperate to provide food for their families.

For those who were apprehended there were local lock-ups where they would be confined until they could be taken before the magistrates and then sent for trial. The St Neots lock-up disappeared many years ago, but a fine example of this type of building which has survived is the Cage, opposite the parish church at Eaton Socon. This was built in 1826 'to confine the refractory'. It never seems to have been used a great deal but has survived various threats of demolition, and today is one of only three that remain within the old county of Huntingdon.

For those caught and convicted punishment was severe and a number of local people, men and women, were sentenced to transportation for periods varying between seven years and life. There were few executions of local people but one case really did hit the national headlines. John Bellingham, who had been born in St Neots in 1776, obtained a job with a Liverpool merchant. This involved him in travelling in various countries, including Russia. When the contracts that he had negotiated there fell through, he was put in prison. On his eventual release he returned to England seeking compensation. This was not forthcoming and, on 11 May 1812, an embittered John Bellingham went to the House of Commons and shot the Prime Minister, Spencer Perceval. He made no attempt to escape and was arrested at the scene of his crime. His trial was pushed through with indecent haste and, within a week of the shooting, Bellingham had been hanged.

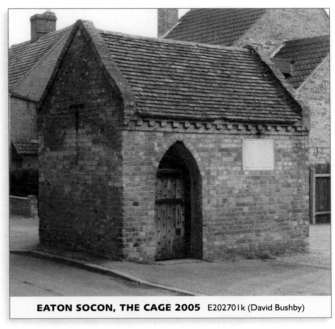

EATON SOCON, THE CAGE 2005 E202701k (David Bushby)

The Cage at Eaton Socon was built in 1826.

JOHN BELLINGHAM ZZZ04680 (Norris Museum)

A TALL STORY

James Toller became known as the Eynesbury Giant, because he could not stop growing. He was probably born in 1795 and died on 4 February 1818. By the age of ten he had reached the height of 5 feet 5 inches. He joined the army in 1813 and served in the 14th Regiment of Light Dragoons. Here he is said to have been noticed by the Duke of York because of his exceptional height. His height proved a problem, though, and he was eventually discharged for being too tall! He then travelled the country, appearing in public exhibitions as a giant. During this time he was apparently presented to the King of Prussia and the Emperor of Russia. Ill-health forced him to return to Eynesbury, where he spent the rest of his short life. When he died he was buried at an unmarked spot inside the parish church for fear of grave robbers. There is no definite proof of his height, but a memorial stone in the church gives it as 8 feet 1 ½ inches.

A PORTRAIT OF JAMES TOLLER, FROM A POSTCARD ORIGINALLY ISSUED IN 1879
ZZZ04681 (Norris Museum)

One way open to young men of escaping from the prevailing working class poverty was to join the army, and many did so. One of these was Matthew Rosamond, who was born at Eaton Socon in 1823. His father died when he was in his teens and, soon after this, he left the village to join the Indian army. On 4 June 1857 he was at Benares when the Indian regiment of which he had become sergeant major mutinied. His inspirational courage on that day led to the award of the coveted Victoria Cross. The citation read: 'This non-commissioned officer volunteered to accompany Lieutenant-Colonel Spottiswoode, commanding the 37th Regiment Bengal Native Infantry, to the right of the lines to set them on fire, with the view of driving out the Sepoys, on the occasion of the outbreak at Benares, on the evening of 4th of June 1857; and

also volunteered, with Sergeant Major Gill of the Loodiana Regiment, to bring off Captain Brown, Pension Paymaster, his wife and infant, and also some others, from a detached bungalow, into the barracks. His conduct was highly meritorious, and he has since been promoted.' When he returned to England on leave in 1861 he stayed at the Bell in Eaton and became involved with the local volunteers, acting as their drill sergeant.

For those who could find no other escape from their poverty there was only the workhouse. The St Neots Poor Law Union had been formed following the Poor Law Amendment Act of 1834. The individual parish workhouses that had existed until then were replaced by one large, new building, erected, after much argument, at Eaton Ford and opened in 1842 with accommodation for up to 338 paupers.

THE FORMER WORKHOUSE 2005 S37707k (David Bushby)

The former St Neots Union Workhouse has now been converted into residential apartments.

The difficulties that affected St Neots and its surrounding villages during the first part of the 19th century were further aggravated by the transport revolution brought about by the development and expansion of the railways in the 1830s and 1840s. Traffic on the Great North Road dwindled to next-to-nothing, and innkeepers and others who had depended on the stagecoaches and other horse-drawn conveyances for their livelihoods found themselves without customers. When the proprietor of the Cock at Eaton Socon was made bankrupt in 1844, he was said to have been a 'victim of the merciless railroad'. This was a cause of particular sadness as the Cock had listed some notable people among its customers. Princess Victoria, as she then was, stopped there briefly in the early 1830s, Lord Torrington was a regular visitor, and William Cowper, poet and hymn-writer, had also lunched there.

By 1846 the number of coaches passing through the area had dwindled to just two a day, and these were only on the local cross-country routes between Bedford and Cambridge. It is not surprising that there was considerable local agitation in favour of the Great Northern Railway, as it became known. This was eventually opened in August 1850. On the opening day local people were given the opportunity of an outing to London or of one to Huntingdon for the races. The railway was an instant success, and within a few weeks an enthusiastic reporter was claiming that the activity of traffic to and from the station gave St Neots the appearance of a bustling town. As well as opening up wider markets to local businesses, it also gave ordinary people the opportunity to travel, with regular excursions to London, Skegness and even further afield.

Alongside the various new developments that were taking place many of the older

A GIFT FOR A QUEEN

Queen Victoria used the Great Northern Railway for her journeys to the north. The royal train did stop at various stations on the line, but never at St Neots. Joseph Barringer, a local baker and noted viticulturist, wanted to present some of his grapes to the queen. On learning that the royal train was stopping at Peterborough in September 1858, he made his way there with a bunch of his best grapes. The local paper reported: 'Our townsman, Mr Barringer, had the honour of presenting Her Majesty, upon her alighting at Peterborough, with a dish of some of his choicest grapes. We understand Her Majesty was most graciously pleased to accept the presentation and that the peculiar fineness of the grapes elicited the marked approval of His Royal Highness, Prince Albert.' Local tradition says that Mr Barringer had placed the grapes on his best silver dish, and was somewhat dismayed to see it disappear on to the train along with the grapes!

trades and crafts continued to be important. Farmers, reliant on the horse for their motive power, resorted to the local smith not only for shoeing but also for the repair and even manufacture of agricultural implements, making the blacksmith's forge a place of great importance in the local economy. The most remarkable of the local smiths was Samuel Pinney, whose premises were in the building known as the Old Plough at Eaton Socon. It is claimed that in 1838 he had made the first all-iron plough in the world; but this is a claim made for various other people as well. Later he turned his hand to something quite different and described himself as an organ

Fact File

According to legend Oliver Cromwell stopped at the forge in Eaton Socon to have his horse shod during the Civil War. There is no evidence for this story but it may well have had its origins in a Parliamentary soldier stopping there at the time of the battle of St Neots in 1648.

builder. How many organs he actually built is unknown but certainly two Pinney organs went into local churches, Eaton Socon parish church and Huntingdon Street Wesleyan Methodist in St Neots.

EATON SOCON, GREAT NORTH ROAD c1960 E202011

The Old Plough, having been a restaurant and tea-room in recent years, is now the Akbar Tandoori.

During the 19th century St Neots itself was to become less dependent on agriculture as other industries developed. A major boost to the town's economy in the early years of the century was the beginning of paper-making. The river mill at the Little Paxton end of St Neots Common was converted from corn milling to paper manufacture by the Fourdrinier brothers in 1804. They had invented important new techniques for producing continuous rolls of paper, rather than the single sheets which were all that could be made until then. This led to St Neots being dubbed the cradle of the paper-making industry. However, the Fourdriniers lacked business know-how, and they were unable to repay the massive loan of £60,000 that they had taken out with Matthew Towgood, a London banker. When the Fourdriniers were forced into bankruptcy in 1808, Matthew Towgood took over the mill. He and his family then ran it for much of the 19th century, after which it was run as a company by a consortium of local business-men.

In a related business, David Stott set up a printing press in St Neots in 1832. He was followed by John Stott, who emigrated to Australia in 1848, leaving the business in the hands of his nephew and former

THE PAPER MILLS 1897 39987

THE RIVER FROM THE BRIDGE 1925 77208

The buildings on the right were Days' Brewery for more than a century.

apprentice, David Tomson. David Tomson, his son Percy Tomson, and Percy's stepson, Colin Lendrum, carried on the business for well over a century in the large building at the east end of St Neots Market Square. It was here that the local paper, the St Neots Advertiser, was printed for many years.

Brewing, already well-established on the old priory site and the Market Square, was given a further impetus by two important take-overs. In 1814 John Day from Bedford took over William Fowler's brewery on the old priory site.

STOUT LABEL ZZZ04682 (Author's Collection)

Day & Son's bottle label for Extra Stout.

57

THE OBELISK

It was John Day of the Priory Brewery who provided the town with its first street light in September 1822. This was made in the form of a cast iron column supporting four lamps. It was erected in the centre of the Market Square (often referred to in earlier times as the Market Hill). It is correctly known as the Day Column but local people generally refer to it as the Obelisk. Today it is a scheduled monument.

THE OBELISK 2005 S37708k (David Bushby)

JAMES PAINE BREWERY 1897 39974x

The entrance to the brewery was through the arch which can be seen behind the horse and wagon.

In 1831 local farmer James Paine, deciding, so it is said, that the beer he gave to his friends was good enough to sell to the public, bought the Market Square brewery, establishing a business that was to become a major employer in the town for more than a century. Later an old flour mill in Bedford Street (then known as Nutter's Lane, after a John Nutter) was added to the business, and this mill was completely rebuilt in 1879. Malt extract works were also established and at one time most of Britain's exports of this product came from St Neots.

The most interesting of the local St Neots businessmen of the 19th century, and the one who exercised by far the greatest influence, was undoubtedly George Bower. He began modestly by taking over an ironmonger's premises on the Market Square in 1850, but soon set up his own manufacturing business, the Vulcan Iron Works. He became involved in the steam revolution and his portable engines were sent all over the country. Bower's main contributions, however, were in the developing gas industry. His inventions and patents were numerous and he installed gas equipment of his own design from household appliances to complete gas works for towns and cities. He exhibited at international exhibitions and sent his equipment abroad, often accompanied by some of his men to oversee the installation. As early as 1851 he installed a gas system at the paper mills that was reckoned to be at least a third more efficient than any previously developed. Over the years he was responsible for installing or extending gasworks in over 1,000 places,

from Kimbolton, the nearest to St Neots, to Mackay in Queensland, Australia, the furthest away.

A PORTABLE STEAM ENGINE ZZZ04683 (Norris Museum)

George Bower's Portable Steam Engine from his 'Gas Engineer's Book of Reference'.

Unfortunately, misfortune or over-ambition led to financial difficulties. In 1876 George Bower filed a petition for bankruptcy but satisfied his creditors that they would be repaid. His business ventures continued on a large scale until 1887, when there was a further petition for bankruptcy. His creditors agreed to allow him another two years, but he managed to keep his business enterprises going well beyond that and was still patenting inventions as late at 1899 when he was 73 years old.

As well as his business activities, Bower became a leading figure in many of the town's organisations and activities. He was a staunch churchman and a Conservative.

In 1881 he was the originator of the St Neots Working Men's Club and became its president. This was the forerunner of the Constitutional Club (now the Conservative Club) in New Street, which was formed in 1894. A number of local events found a venue in the grounds of his long-time home, The Shrubbery. These included the St Neots Horticultural Society's annual show, and the church Sunday School annual treat. Tennis tournaments were also held there when this became a popular game in the 1880s.

George Bower also made a major contribution to the expansion of St Neots. He had acquired the land on which Avenue Road now stands and in 1886 he offered plots of this for building. Many of the houses there today go back to this development, while others date from 1896 when a further 26 plots were sold.

As those businesses had developed that were to exercise an important influence on St Neots throughout the 19th century and, in some cases, well beyond, other important changes were also taking place. Local government was taking its first faltering steps. St Neots had never acquired a charter in the way that other places in the county, like Huntingdon and Godmanchester, had done. As local control had moved from the manor courts to the vestry, the town was being run in the same way as any village of the time. Then, in 1819, the St Neots Paving and Lighting Act established commissioners to deal with these aspects of the town's development, and to be responsible for such

amenities as street lighting and paving. The town commissioners were an autocratic self-perpetuating body, which, despite some early achievements, never quite succeeded in providing the services to which people increasingly felt they were entitled. These included such things as sewage disposal and water supply, both of which were woefully inadequate, but neither of which was dealt with efficiently until the 20th century. This was despite the vigorous attempts of George Bower, who inevitably became one of the commissioners, to acquire decent amenities for the town.

The town commissioners at St Neots and the vestry at Eynesbury both proved unequal to the task of providing anything like reasonable living standards for the poor. At Eynesbury conditions were unimaginably bad, and at one inquest - a case of infant mortality in November 1870 - it was claimed that many dwellings in the village were worse than the worst slums in London. An inquiry was held in 1875 to look at the local government of the area, and this decided that St Neots and Eynesbury should be joined under the control of an elected Local Board which would replace the vestry at Eynesbury and the Town Commissioners as the instrument of local government for the area. The first election for this took place in 1876 and George Bower, inevitably perhaps, became its chairman. While the Local Board achieved a good deal in its nineteen-year existence, it still failed to tackle some basic issues, such as sanitation and the water supply. It was replaced by St Neots Urban District Council at the end of 1894.

Religion continued to play an important part in many people's lives. The middle part of the century here, as elsewhere, was the period of church restorations, and extensive work was undertaken at the parish churches of St Neots (1844), Eynesbury (1857-58) and Eaton Socon (1867). Extra seating was provided in that heyday of Victorian church attendance, and the emphasis of worship was significantly changed as the former musicians of the singing gallery were moved to seats in the chancel and became the choir.

Nonconformity also flourished and this gave rise to a flurry of church building activity. No longer did the nonconformists feel the need to hide behind plain, unadorned, and generally unobtrusive structures. The Wesleyan Methodists gave their simple, barn-like building in Huntingdon Street a fine new front in 1867, with conspicuous twin towers and an ornate porch.

Nowhere, though, is the Victorian love of ornamentation and display of wealth better illustrated than in the building of a new Congregational church (now United Reformed) in 1888. Its spire, towering up as a local landmark, made it far more conspicuous and ostentatious than the 18th

ST NEOTS CHURCH, THE INTERIOR 1925 77211

century Old Meeting, which was retained as a meeting hall.

There were other nonconformist churches, all of which flourished for a while but have since closed, although the buildings remain. A Gospel Hall was erected in New Street in 1867. This became a shoe factory in the 1940s and is now Clover Office Supplies. A General Baptist chapel was built in East Street in 1873 but since 1931 has been St Joseph's

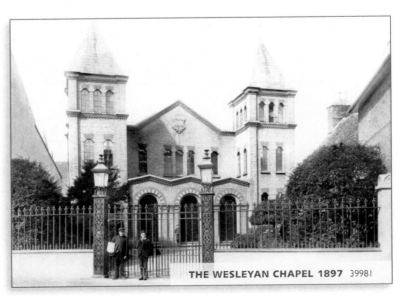

THE WESLEYAN CHAPEL 1897 39981

THE CONGREGATIONAL CHURCH 1897 39982

Roman Catholic Church. The Salvation Army became established in the town and a citadel was built at the Cross on the corner of High Street and Church Street, which opened in December 1891. After regular services ended the building was used for some years as a Christian bookshop, but was eventually sold and is now a clothes shop.

As the 19th century progressed the people of St Neots gained a greater awareness of what it meant to be townspeople, and what amenities a town should be expected to have. This led to the erection of several important secular buildings. In 1839 local auctioneer William Medland built a large new premises adjoining St Neots Bridge, and these, at first known as the New Rooms and later as the Public Rooms, became an important venue for concerts, entertainments and plays. St Neots Gas Company was formed late in 1845 and the town was lit by gas for the first time at the beginning of September 1846, making it a much more wholesome place at night. Law and order became better established with the introduction of the county police force and the building of a police house, station, and magistrates' court in New Street in 1859.

NEW STREET 1925 77205

The magistrates' court, on the right, now houses St Neots Museum, which opened in December 1995.

A Corn Exchange Company was formed and in 1863 erected a fine, ornate building, with an elegant cupola. Not only was it used as a corn market on Thursdays, but it became the regular venue for plays, concerts, and other entertainments, largely replacing the Public Rooms as the major centre for local events as well as for the increasing number of visiting companies of actors and entertainers. The Corn Exchange was also to house the Literary Institute, which was formed in 1863, and became an important organisation in the social and cultural life of the town.

New schools were also built to meet the requirements of providing at least an elementary education for all. In Eynesbury and St Neots these were voluntary schools,

THE CORN EXCHANGE 1863 ZZZ04684 (Norris Museum)

built and run by the churches. Eaton Socon, on the other hand, had to elect a school board in 1872 to ensure that the village had an adequate number of elementary school places.

SCHOOL LANE c1960 E202021

Eaton Socon School was originally built as a Church of England school in 1860. It was later transferred to Eaton Socon School Board and in 1903 became a council school. The buildings, no longer used as a school, were damaged by a serious fire in 1981 and subsequently demolished.

Just three of these 19th century buildings remain today; the former Church Boys' School in Church Walk, built in 1860, is one. The others are to be found at Eynesbury, and this is interesting as there are three periods of school building on the one site. The first, right on the road, is very small, and there is still the bellcote to be seen above it where the school bell, cast in 1855, once hung. This would have been the infant school opened by the Rev William Maule in January 1856. Behind it is the National School that was erected in 1868, and behind that is today's school, which was opened in 1964.

The neighbourhood was also important for its private schools, of which there were a large

Fact File

Otto Madden, a pupil at The School, went on to become a top jockey, winning the jockeys' championship four times between 1898 and 1904. In 1898 he rode Jeddah to success in the Derby at 100-1, the longest odds winner in the history of the race. He enjoyed further classic success when he rode Challacombe to victory in the St Ledger in 1905.

number. Two were particularly important for providing a sound middle-class education; one for boys at Eaton Socon, simply known as The School, and the other for girls, Prospect House School, in New Street, St Neots.

THE EARLIEST SURVIVING SCHOOL BUILDINGS AT EYNESBURY 2005 S37709k (David Bushby)

THE GREAT NORTH ROAD c1960 E202024

If improved educational opportunities were one important development for the working classes of the area, another was the establishment of a local Co-operative Society. This began at Eaton Socon in 1882, but in 1886 members held a meeting in St Neots to urge the establishment of a branch there. As a result a shop was built in Huntingdon Street in 1887, and Eaton Socon became a branch of St Neots, with a further branch being established in Eynesbury. The St Neots building remains and the date and Co-op motto are still there, although it is no longer a Co-op shop.

The river, important for both business and leisure activities, has also had a less beneficial effect on the area. It would be impossible to write about St Neots in the 19th century without giving some description of the impact of flooding on the town and neighbourhood.

Few years seem to have escaped completely and sometimes there were several floods in a season. In January 1815 a Mr Thorn had lost more than 50 ewes, swept away when a sudden thaw caused the river to flood. The flood of 30 October 1823 was exceptional and regarded as possibly the worst since that recorded as having deluged the town in 1579. It became the benchmark by which other floods in the 19th century were judged. When the water was at its highest, the parish church, never known to have been flooded, had two feet of water in it. The walls of the town bridge were broken down and the main arch damaged, while the bridge at the paper mills was destroyed completely. The Regent stagecoach, bound for the north, became stuck at Eaton Socon and the passengers had to be ferried to their inn by boat. People were rowing boats and even brewery tubs on the

HUNTINGDON STREET 2005 S3771 0k (David Bushby)

The original Co-operative Society shop in Huntingdon Street. In the apex of the roof are the date, 1887, and the motto 'Unity is Strength'.

Market Square, trying to salvage goods that were floating about.

Fortunately there is no record of the floods ever having caused the direct loss of human life, but they did lead to conditions that were not only uncomfortable, but also extremely unhealthy. In November 1880 James Bennett, long-serving headmaster at St Neots Boys' Charity School, wrote that cases of typhoid fever had occurred among children, 'owing to flood water in the houses of the low part of the town'. Some of the worst floods occurred during the 1890s, and they were particularly severe in 1891, 1894 and 1897.

If floods were a regular and unwelcome aspect of life in St Neots, the annual fairs were looked forward to eagerly. The three-day St Neots Holy Thursday Fair, the most important one of the year, was often referred to simply as the Great Fair. In its heyday sheep were penned all along the High Street, while horses and cattle were offered for sale on the Common. The Market Square was taken up by the various stalls and attractions of a pleasure fair. In its earlier days and until well past the middle of the 19th century it was very much a local, family occasion. In May 1863 the mistress of the Church Girls' School wrote that several pupils were absent, assisting their parents in preparations for the fair. Later in the century it became the preserve of the large travelling fairs, such as Thurstons. The local middle classes came to look down on the pleasure fair as an event fit only for the large numbers of unsophisticated country people, as they regarded them, that it attracted into the town.

For many years the annual fairs were important for the buying and selling of animals, but the volume of business declined during the century. A more regular means of sale was looked for and this was established by 1864 when Ennals & Son began periodic stock sales. A weekly cattle market eventually found its home in New Street and, after passing through several hands, was acquired by S V Ekins just after the turn of the century, in 1902.

One of the important developments as the 19th century progressed was the growth in sport and leisure activities. Cricket had made an impact early on and was played on the common from 1816, if not earlier. Swimming would have taken place in the river from earliest times, but Victorian respectability came to look on this with some alarm as participants generally swam naked: there were various warnings about indecent bathing. The situation was regularised when the Urban District Council provided bathing sheds with paid attendants at both St Neots and Eynesbury.

For many years St Neots has been a strong centre of rowing and its oarsmen and women have brought many trophies back to the town. The first rowing club was formed in 1860 but this failed after only a short while.

A new one was established in 1873 under the chairmanship of the Rev William Maule, the charismatic rector of Eynesbury, a former rowing blue and winner of the prestigious diamond sculls at Henley.

Weather permitting, the winter sport, was skating, either on the river itself or on ice on the flooded Lammas Meadow. This attracted

arge numbers of people and, when the river was frozen over in February 1855, it was stimated that nearly 500 people were on the ce each day. In the severe winter of 1890-91 t Neots Skating Association was formed, nd a cup presented to be held by the winner f the open men's event. Bandy, a form of ce hockey, also became popular. This was encouraged by Charles G Tebbutt, who had set up in business in St Neots in 1889. He was a skater of international renown and, as captain of the Bury Fen bandy team, not only helped popularise the game locally, but also introduced it on to the Continent.

Football gained popularity in the late 1860s. It had been played regularly in Eaton

THE RIVER c1955 S37023

Socon from about 1860 onwards, but only within the village. The first public match, between Bedfordshire and Huntingdonshire, took place there in November 1867. It lasted for two hours with a ten-minute interval and ended 1-1. This was not soccer as it is played today, rather something of a cross between soccer and rugby. It was not until September 1880 that St Neots Football Club, which had been founded two years previously, decided that in future it would play its matches in accordance with Association rules.

Other sports rose to prominence in the later years of the century and none more so than cycling. There were several local men who manufactured bicycles, the most notable being Edward Ireland, maker of the Defiance. These were ridden competitively by E J 'Josh' Bass who won races on them across the country, including the prestigious National Cycling Union's 25-mile race at Northampton in 1900. There was also at that time a cycle track in Priory Park, which G Fydell Rowley had had improved to National Cycling Union standards in 1898. This was used on various occasions, such as the Primrose League's Easter Monday Sports, which were held there.

The game of hockey was at one time regarded locally as being quite disreputable and was described in 1879 as a game 'played in the street

Fact File

Each year the Cycling Club used a tandem for its paper chase. The hares would set off on it, and after three minutes would be pursued by the rest of the club until they were caught. This was to work up an appetite for the club dinner in the evening!

FRANK DAY ZZZ04685 (From Frank Day's photograph album, used by permission of Jean Hawkins)

Frank Day and another member of St Neots Cycling Club in Priory Park.

y boys and hobbledehoys'. As an organised sport, it began locally with a highly successful women's team at Eaton Socon in 1898. This was followed by the formation of St Neots Men's Hockey Club in 1901 and regular matches were soon being played.

Golf, too, became popular and a club was established in 1890. As with many of the other sports, it was played initially on the Common. Unlike most other sports it was open equally to men and women players.

In the changing world of the late 19th and early 20th centuries there was a growing leisure industry, and there were various moves to attract visitors to St Neots, often organised by the Town Attractions Committee. The introduction of cheap day return tickets

encouraged many Londoners to visit the town and enjoy a leisurely day by the river, and these visits proved lucrative for many local traders.

The discovery of a mineral spring near the paper mills in the early 1890s led to a consortium being formed to create a spa, and to promote St Neots as a spa town. St Neots Spa was launched with great enthusiasm on Whit Monday 1895, but the initial optimism quickly waned and the spa only continued with a struggle, in little more than name and without any of the trappings or amenities of a pump room or spa gardens. However, spa water was bottled and sold under the name Neotia by the local firm of Jordan and Addington for many years.

THE MILL c1965 S37039

The platform that was built for the spa can still be seen over the wall on the right just beyond Mill Cottage.

St Neots has seldom hit the national news headlines but it did so in 1895 as a result of a serious railway accident. On 10 November the 11.30pm night 'Scotsman' from King's Cross was passing St Neots at about 60 miles an hour at 12.30am, when a rail broke. The engine and its front five coaches stayed on the track but the back four coaches were derailed and crashed with tremendous force into some loaded coal wagons. Two people died and several others were seriously injured. Undoubtedly, had the train been full, the death toll would have been much higher, but fortunately it was only carrying 27 passengers.

Despite this setback the Great Northern Railway went from strength to strength and

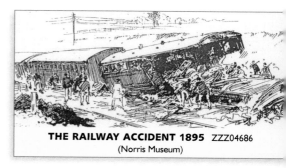

THE RAILWAY ACCIDENT 1895 ZZZ04686
(Norris Museum)

This drawing of the St Neots railway accident was used in an advertisement to encourage rail travellers to take out insurance before embarking on their journey.

in 1898 the number of tracks was doubled. The original St Neots station was demolished and a new station built, parts of which still remain. The major feature, though, a large granary, was destroyed by fire in May 1968.

ST NEOTS STATION BOOKING OFFICE 2005 S37711k (David Bushby)

St Neots Station booking office dates from 1898.

THE ST NEOTS POISONER

The settled and peaceful world of late 19th century St Neots was disturbed in 1898 by a notorious murder case. On 7 January Annie Holmes (38), a widow living in St Neots, died in violent pain, having apparently taken a powder which she had received through the post. She was a cousin of Walter Horsford (26) and had been having an affair with him. At the opening of the inquest he denied sending anything to her or having any relationship with her. Two days later, though, he was arrested on a charge of perjury and, when the inquest ended on 14 January, a verdict of wilful murder by Horsford was returned. Annie Holmes's body was exhumed and found to contain a significant amount of strychnine. After appearing before the St Neots Bench on some five occasions Walter Horsford was committed for trial at Huntingdon Assizes on the charge of murder. Here he was found to be guilty, and was executed at Cambridge on 28th June 1898.

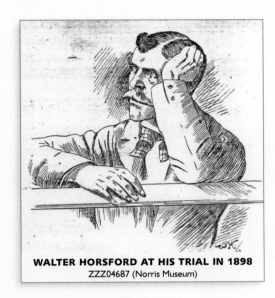

WALTER HORSFORD AT HIS TRIAL IN 1898
ZZZ04687 (Norris Museum)

Throughout the 19th century St Neots was fiercely royalist. Royal occasions were marked by appropriate events or celebrations. Among the highlights was the wedding of the Prince of Wales in 1863. When the royal couple were in the town on their way to and from the Duke of Manchester's home at Kimbolton Castle in 1868, it was treated as a great occasion and the townspeople turned out in force to cheer them.

The two jubilees of Queen Victoria's reign, in 1887 and 1897, also aroused considerable excitement. At the 1887 jubilee people subscribed to purchase a town clock which, unsurprisingly, became known as the Jubilee Clock. This was hung on the High Street side of the Corn Exchange. Also in 1887 Dr John Jewel Evans, who had a private museum in his home, Brook House, offered it to the town. The Literary Institute agreed to house this in its rented rooms in the Corn Exchange, and so the Victoria Museum was established.

As well as the Jubilee Clock and Victoria Museum, Jubilee Day itself was marked by a series of events involving the whole community. Eynesbury and Little Paxton

HIGH STREET 1925 77213

joined with St Neots to make it a memorable occasion. Houses were decorated throughout the town, with householders trying to outdo one another. There were sports on the Common and on the Market Square, while there was a treat for the children, each of whom received a jubilee mug. In the evening a banquet at the Corn Exchange culminated in the formal opening of the Victoria Museum.

In 1897 no public monuments were erected to mark the jubilee and the Urban District Council resisted a suggestion that Avenue Road should be renamed Victoria

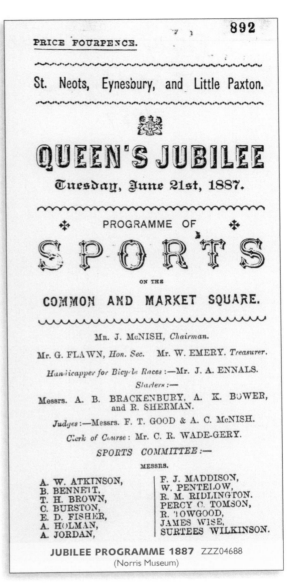

PRICE FOURPENCE.

892

St. Neots, Eynesbury, and Little Paxton.

QUEEN'S JUBILEE

Tuesday, June 21st, 1887.

PROGRAMME OF

SPORTS

ON THE

COMMON AND MARKET SQUARE.

Mr. J. McNISH, *Chairman.*

Mr. G. FLAWN, *Hon. Sec.*   Mr. W. EMERY, *Treasurer.*

*Handicapper for Bicycle Races :—*Mr. J. A. ENNALS.

Starters :—

Messrs. A. B. BRACKENBURY, A. K. BOWER, and R. SHERMAN.

*Judges :—*Messrs. F. T. GOOD & A. C. McNISH.

Clerk of Course : Mr. C. R. WADE-GERY.

SPORTS COMMITTEE :—

MESSRS.

A. W. ATKINSON,	F. J. MADDISON,
B. BENNETT,	W. PENTELOW,
T. H. BROWN,	R. M. RIDLINGTON,
C. BURSTON,	PERCY C. TOMSON,
E. D. FISHER,	R. TOWGOOD,
A. HOLMAN,	JAMES WISE,
A. JORDAN,	SURTEES WILKINSON.

JUBILEE PROGRAMME 1887 ZZZ04688
(Norris Museum)

Crescent. An ambitious programme of celebrations and entertainments was undertaken, with pony races and cycle, athletic, and rural sports. In the evening dancing on the Market Square ended with a bonfire and fireworks display.

At the end of the 19th century, a church service was held 'to bury the old century and usher in the new'. St Neots and Eynesbury people no doubt felt that there was much from the past on which they could reflect with pride, and also that they had good grounds to look forward to the future with optimism.

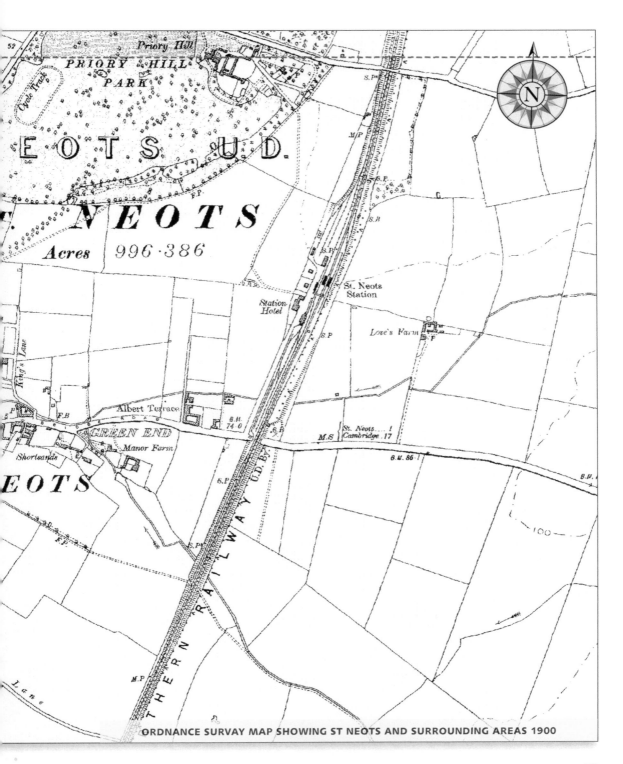

ORDNANCE SURVAY MAP SHOWING ST NEOTS AND SURROUNDING AREAS 1900

CHAPTER FOUR

A SMALL TOWN
GROWS UP

ST NEOTS FROM THE AIR c1955 S37013

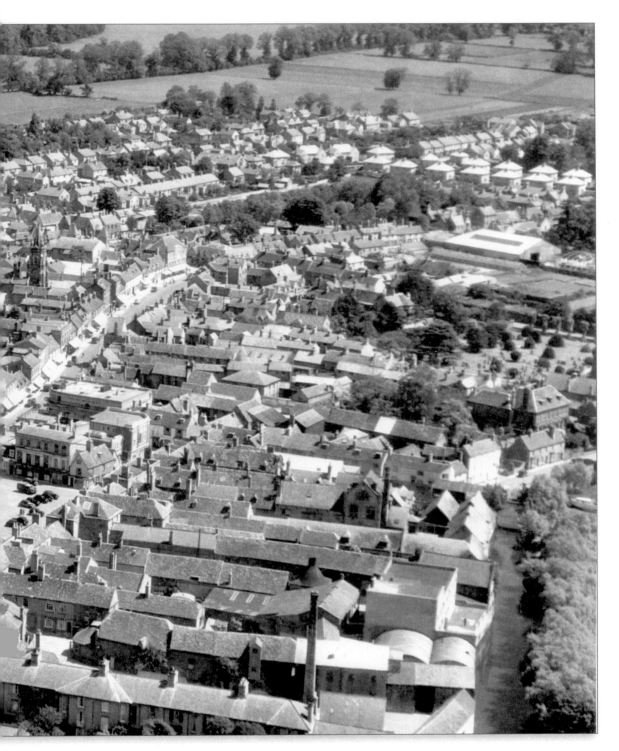

THE NEW century saw a renewed burst of building activity. The town, while remaining essentially small and with only a minimal growth in population, continued to spread eastwards. Shaftesbury Avenue was built up in 1904. On the north side of the Market Square Barclays Bank, which had taken over the local bank in 1896, erected an imposing new building in 1901. William Seward, a major businessman in the town during the early years of the century, built a new boot and shoe shop in the High Street in 1901 and followed this up with other new premises in 1904. The Royal Oak (now the Halifax Bank) was rebuilt in 1903. All this, together with Charles Wren's new fish shop in 1905, helped give the town centre a fresher and more modern face.

Although so many of the old St Neots family businesses have disappeared, one that began in the early years of the 20th century still flourishes. In 1906 Frank Brittain opened a furniture shop in Eaton Ford. He moved into the building on St Neots Market Square that had once been the post office in April 1914 and subsequently into the High Street, where the present shop is still run by members of the family.

HIGH STREET c1955 S37007

The family businesses seen here have now all closed.

NOTED SHOP FOR YARMOUTH BLOATERS.
ALL KINDS OF FISH WHEN IN SEASON.

CHARLES WREN,
Wholesale & Retail Fishmonger
AND FRUITERER,
High Street, ST. NEOTS.

FRESH FISH DAILY FROM THE COAST.

HOT FISH & CHIPPED POTATOES, Wednesday, Thursday, Friday, and Saturday nights, from 7.30 to 10.
Filleted Haddock a Speciality.   Houseboats supplied daily.

ESTABLISHED OVER 70 YEARS.

PICKLED TONGUES.
PICKLED PORK.
SALT BEEF a Speciality.

JOHN BARTLETT & SON,
Family Butchers,
HUNTINGDON STREET AND SOUTH STREET,
ST. NEOTS.

T. L. WILLIAMSON,
Wheelwright, Van, Cart,
: and Coach Builder, :

THE PRIORY, ST. NEOTS, HUNTS.

Repairs and Painting in all its Branches.
MOTOR BODIES BUILT TO ORDER.

RUBBER TYRES : FITTED. :

WORKMANSHIP : GUARANTEED. :

Every Description of Light and Heavy Vehicles built to Order.

JOHN LYNN,
General Furnishing and Agricultural Ironmonger,

GUNS AND AMMUNITION.
REPAIRS OF ALL KINDS.

LICENSED TO SELL METHYLATED SPIRIT.

High Street, ST. NEOTS.

THE BEST SOUVENIR OF
THE TOWN IS A PIECE OF
GOSS   PORCELAIN
WITH ST. NEOTS ARMS AND ALFRED JEWEL.

TO BE OBTAINED ONLY OF

A. G. BARRITT,
JEWELLER,
High Street, ST. NEOTS.

A large selection of Jewellery and Silver Goods for Presents.

SILVER SOUVENIR SPOONS.

B. BAKER,
Baker and

Pure Home Made
Bread.

Currant Bread, and

Whole-Meal Bread.

Confectioner,

Russell Street,
ST. NEOTS.

:-:   FAMILIES SUPPLIED DAILY.   :-:

Advertisements for well-known St Neots family businesses from the early 20th century ZZZ04689-94 (Author's Collection

After years of resistance and delay, just before the end of the 19th century mains water had at last been brought to the town when the St Neots Water Company was formed. This had not proved to be a successful commercial venture and had lacked the support of the Urban District Council. The result was that the company had to be wound up in 1906 and, after protracted negotiations, the Urban District Council acquired it for £9,000 in 1907.

Shortly before this the council had found it necessary to take on another responsibility, that of the Victoria Museum. The Literary Institute had been struggling for some years and eventually closed in 1910. Before this, in 1905, it had

decided that it could no longer maintain the museum and the council reluctantly agreed to take it on.

The changes that were taking place in those early years of the 20th century are nowhere better illustrated than by the increasing impact of the motor car on the life of the area. As the Great North Road passed through the centre of Eaton Socon and a main east-west road passed directly through St Neots, this was inevitable. But St Neots gained a special notoriety as it was the local bench here that had the responsibility of dealing with speeding drivers caught in the infamous Buckden speed trap, reputedly the worst in the country. G Fydell Rowley, Chairman of

AN EARLY MOTORING MISHAP ON THE GREAT NORTH ROAD

As the number of motor-cars on the roads increased, the St Neots area became notorious for accidents. Many of these occurred at the crossroads at Cross Hall as there was no idea in the early motoring days that the traffic on the Great North Road should have the right of way. It was, though, the stretch of the Great North Road in Eaton Socon parish known as Dirt House Hill that was particularly dangerous, and in the period before it was eventually bypassed there were no less than thirteen fatalities in three years.

A RIVER VIEW 1925 77207

This view includes one of Mr Gill's houseboats.

THE GREAT NORTH ROAD ZZZ04695 (From Frank Day's photograph album, used by permission of Jean Hawkins)

the St Neots Bench for many years, had a great distrust of the motor-car. Some of his comments proved to be only too true, as in April 1903 when he expressed his belief that 'one of these days a motor-car driver will be charged with manslaughter'.

If the motor-car was the sign of things to come, the river continued to be one of St Neots' greatest attractions. An entrepreneur who did do much to promote the town during the first part of the 20th century was Charles Gill, who developed what is now the marina. He was a master craftsman and a fine carver; and some of his work can still be seen in Eynesbury church. But his most interesting venture began in

BREARLEY'S LANDING STAGE c1955 S37022

For many years this was known locally as Houseboat Corner.

901 when he built a houseboat, 'Ouse Lily', and let it out to holiday-makers.

Other houseboats followed, and the juncture of Hen Brook and the Ouse became known as Houseboat Corner.

River and houseboat concerts, organised by Mr Gill, did much to enhance the social life of the town, and helped to develop good

relationships between the holidaymakers and the townspeople. Strangely, perhaps, this holiday business actually increased during the First World War years, as people who had previously travelled abroad looked for places nearer home. St Neots, with its river and quaint market town charm, proved to be attractive.

One major new leisure facility was provided with the opening of the Pavilion cinema. Films had been shown for some years in the old Public Rooms, but this venue was not particularly well adapted to the purpose. The Corn Exchange Company had been struggling for a number of years and finally went into voluntary liquidation. After an abortive attempt by the Urban District Council to buy the premises as a public hall and council offices, it was acquired by Charles Alfred James, who converted it into the Pavilion cinema, and this opened in March 1916.

There was a strong military presence in the town during the years of the First World War, as its large market square and extensive common proved ideal places for military activities. At one time the guns of the Highland Brigade, Royal Artillery, were parked on the Market Square when the brigade spent the first winter of the war in the town before going to France. Large numbers of local men enlisted in the Huntingdonshire Cyclist Battalion, which was sent to patrol parts of the east coast, but many of them were subsequently drafted into various regiments and sent to France. There were Red Cross hospitals at both

St Neots and Eaton Socon, and wounded soldiers were often in evidence around the town. The war years provided local women here, as elsewhere, with new opportunities. As far as the St Neots area was concerned these were mainly in agricultural work, but the appointment that attracted the most notice was that of a Mrs Phillips as the town's first postwoman.

Many local activities did manage to continue during the war years, and some new things were introduced to the area by soldiers who were stationed locally. It was two Welsh teams, for instance, that played the first known game of rugby union in the town. All the bustle and activity of the coming and going of troops and visitors did little to cover the gloom that descended on the neighbourhood as news of the deaths of local men, many of them not yet 20 years old, became an all too regular feature. It was, then, a sombre community that welcomed the end of the war and gave lavishly to provide memorials to the dead. The war memorials in the three parishes record the names of 182 men who had died. In St Neots more than £1,000 was raised to recast and rehang the church bells as a tribute to the town's war dead. Later more money was contributed to erect the public memorial, which stands in Church Walk.

THE BOATYARD c1960 S37027

The footbridge over Hen Brook had originally been constructed by Charles Gill in 1903.

EATON SOCON, THE GREEN AND MEMORIAL c1960 E202015

Eaton Socon war memorial was unveiled on Palm Sunday, 1921.

It has been said that the history of a community can often be traced by its fires. St Neots had escaped lightly in the past, with no more than the occasional cottage fire or more frequent farm stack fire, but the years either side of the First World War saw a number of major fires. Paine & Co's brewery on the Market Square (1905) and its flour mill in Bedford Street (1909), the paper mills (1912) and Jordan and Addington's seed warehouse (1913) were among the major business premises to be gutted. The Pavilion cinema - the former Corn Exchange - was destroyed by fire in 1929 and, most dramatic of all, Eaton Socon church was reduced to little more than a heap of rubble in February 1930.

It is a sad reflection on the penny-pinching attitudes of local government that it took fires like these to expose the inadequacies of the equipment that the fire brigade had to work with. It was only following severe criticism after the Paines' fire in 1905 that the Urban District Council agreed to the purchase of a second-hand steamer, which was to give good service for many years. Not until 1934, though, did the town acquire a modern motor fire engine.

All the buildings that had been destroyed by these various fires were rebuilt. The new Paine & Co mill in Bedford Street, with its tall tower, was a particularly impressive building. This was erected in 1910 by the well-known St Neots firm of George Wrycroft & Sons. The firm was responsible for a good deal of the new building in the town in the first part of the 20th century, including the paper mills, the post office in New Street in 1913 and the Jordan and Addington seed warehouses in 1914.

The main buildings at the paper mills had been reduced to heaps of masonry and twisted machinery by the fire. Such, though, was the determination to rebuild and restart production that within a year paper was again being produced.

The Pavilion cinema was also rebuilt, but without the graceful cupola that had been such a distinctive feature of the old Corn Exchange. Of great interest here was the fate of the Jubilee Clock, the works of which had been damaged beyond repair. The case had survived intact, though, and it was duly reinstated in its old position, but with electric rather than mechanical works.

The greatest rebuilding feat was that at Eaton Socon, where a new church rose from the ashes in as near its original form as was possible. This was largely due to the determination of the vicar, the Rev Edgar Higham, and the architectural genius of Professor (later Sir) Albert Richardson. The new building was dedicated by the Bishop of St Albans on Saturday 25 June 1932.

THE PAPER MILLS 1925 77209

EATON SOCON CHURCH c1960 E202013

Fact File

The famous composer, Sir Edward Elgar, belonged to the same London Club as Professor Richardson, the architect of the new church at Eaton Socon, and he invited Elgar to write a set of chimes for the new church clock. Unfortunately Elgar's composition did not work well on the Eaton Socon set-up, and those of the church organist, Surtees Wilkinson, were chosen instead. It is said that Elgar and Richardson never spoke to one another again!

Just after the end of the First World War the town suffered a serious loss with the closure of Days' Brewery. When Frank Day died at the early age of 56 in June 1919 there was no family member to continue the business, so it had to close. The brewery buildings were taken over by the firm of Jordan and Addington, but they were no longer used for brewing.

At the sale of Frank Day's estates, the Priory garden was acquired by St Neots & District Recreation Club Company and developed for various sports, especially bowls which gained great popularity in the area in the years immediately following the end of the war. Interest in the Recreation Club Company itself declined during the 1930s. In 1939 St Neots Bowling Club acquired its assets and with them control of the whole site.

As the town began to recover from the effects of the war, the Urban District Council turned its attention to providing the new housing that the town needed. This resulted in 1921 in the first council house estates being built off the Cambridge Road, just before the railway bridge in St Neots, and off Berkley Street in Eynesbury.

It was in a house in Ferrers Avenue, as the new Eynesbury estate had been called, that quads were born to Walter and Doris Miles on 28 November 1935. This was the first known live birth of quads, certainly nationally and possibly worldwide, and was an event that propelled the St Neots area into the national spotlight. The then-popular Daily Sketch secured exclusive rights to their story. Cow & Gate sponsored them and could advertise that the St Neots Quads, as they became known, were being fed on their products. Soon after their birth they had been moved to St Neots, first to their doctor's house, The Shrubbery, in Church Street, and later to a large house, The Gables, in New Street, where people came from far and wide to watch them at play in their specially-built nursery.

EYNESBURY, FERRERS AVENUE 2005 S37712k (David Bushby)

THE QUADS, BORN IN 1935 ZZZ04696

One of a whole series of postcards of the quads that was issued. Paul, Ernest, Ann and Michael are seen with their older brother, Gordon, on a visit to a pet lamb they had been given.

Fact File

On Wednesday, 9 March 2005, three of the quads, Paul, Ernest and Ann, were back in St Neots to unveil a blue plaque on their former home in New Street. Michael was unable to attend as he lives in South Africa.

This house
was home to the
ST NEOTS QUADS
Born at Ferrers Avenue, Eynesbury
on 28th November 1935
to Mr and Mrs Miles,
they attracted national interest.

A nursery was added to this house by
H F Bull & Sons and opened by
the Minister of Health
on 30th June 1936

THE ST NEOTS QUADS' PLAQUE 2005
ZZZ04697 (David Bushby)

The business face of St Neots was beginning to change during these years. Although it was still based largely on small, family concerns, some national chains, such as International Stores and F W Woolworth, did become established. Also St Neots Co-operative Society moved on to the High Street in 1930, acquiring the old Assembly Room premises. These are still occupied by the Co-op today, although now as part of the Westgate Group.

Of the many changes in the late 1920s and the 1930s, electricity, provided by the BC&H (Bedfordshire, Cambridgeshire and Huntingdonshire Electricity Company), brought its benefits to many, while radio helped to broaden people's horizons, with significant events being broadcast publicly on the Market Square. There was also a great feeling of pride in the town's successes during these years; whether in its sports teams, or in the Eynesbury and St Neots Silver Prize Band under its conductor Horace Catmull, or in the gold medals won for pork pies by John Rayns Smith, or in prizes for bakery by W S Shepherd. All these were heralded as signs of the town's growing prestige.

There was no such feeling of pride about the town's Victoria Museum. It had been inadequately housed ever since the loss of the Corn Exchange premises, and many council members came to see it as nothing but a nuisance. In 1932 it was offered to the newly-formed Norris Museum at St Ives. This offer was accepted and the best local items were taken there, where fortunately they are still preserved today.

HIGH STREET FROM THE CROSS c1965 S37070

Many of the specimens in the Victoria Museum were stuffed birds and animals, and some of these were retained until 1950 when they were finally disposed of. Some of the best had been preserved by St Neots' own taxidermist, William Chamberlain. He had worked from a small terraced cottage in Russell Street from the 1880s until his death in 1901. When he was working on a particularly interesting specimen, local people were always invited to call in and view his handiwork.

As elsewhere, the late 1920s and early 930s were often difficult ones economically. Nowhere was this effect felt more strongly hat at the paper mills, where a severe downturn in the industry caused grave problems. The noted firm of Wiggins, Teape & Co of Dover took over the business in 930 but closed it down two years later.

Another loss in the 1930s was the facility for river bathing from the sheds at Eynesbury and St Neots. There had been concerns about the deteriorating quality of the river water for some years and the analysis taken in June 1939 showed that it was no longer safe, so the sheds were closed and later demolished. At the time this was the least of people's concerns, as preparations for war were increasing rapidly.

THE RIVER c1965 S37036

The years of the Second World War were hectic ones in St Neots. Evacuees spilled into the area in their hundreds, but generally settled well into their temporary homes and contributed much to the life of the local community. More was seen of the war this time, as various planes, enemy and friendly, crashed or were brought down in the locality. As St Neots was ringed by airfields, the skies were often filled with the throb of engines. Again, large numbers of service personnel were in evidence in the town, attending various functions, dances in the Public Rooms or films at the cinema. The latter was, somewhat controversially, allowed to open on Sundays. There was also a prisoner of war camp in Huntingdon Street, which was not finally closed until 1948.

The war years brought one major boost for local industry with the reopening of the paper mills. Because of the frequent bombing of Dover, Wiggins, Teape & Co decided to move their operations from there to St Neots and the first paper for nine years was produced in June 1941. Eventually, with three machines running non-stop, 110 tons of paper were being produced each week.

Immediately after the end of the war though, there was a period when the town really did seem to struggle, and many old organisations and institutions never recovered. Among the casualties was the Eynesbury & St Neots Silver Prize Band; while the various feasts and statutes either died out or lost their old traditions and simply became modern fun fairs. Housing was often inadequate, with a great deal of overcrowding, and it took many years for the Urban District Council to resolve this problem. Matters were not helped by a severe winter in 1946-47 with blizzards nd heavy snow. This was followed by the worst floods for more than a hundred years, which struck in March 1947 and left much of St Neots, Eynesbury, and Eaton under water. There was widespread devastation, and a major relief operation was launched which attracted help from a wide area, even from as far away as South Africa.

Spirits were lifted in 1948 when the prestigious National Rowing Association's All-England Championship 'Fours' event was held on the river at St Neots. It was decided to celebrate the occasion by holding a week-long carnival in the town, and an ambitious programme was organised. This was to prove the forerunner of the annual St Neots Carnival, which, despite various ups and downs, has taken place ever since. In the course of more than 50 years it has not only given a great deal of pleasure but has also raised thousands of pounds for local organisations and charities.

As the town began to get on its feet again there were several major projects and developments providing people with new or improved amenities. Of major importance was a modern sewerage scheme, which had been proposed in the 1930s, but this had to be postponed in 1939 after hitting numerous problems. Further difficulties were put in the way of the scheme in the period after the end of the war, including that of obtaining grants in a period of national financial stringency. The situation became so serious that the future expansion of the town seemed under threat. Eventually in 1954 the last difficulties were overcome and the work was able to go ahead.

Another scheme that aroused great interest in the mid-1950s, and helped extend the town's shopping facilities, was the creation of the arcade. Two empty shops on the north side of the Market Square were scheduled for demolition. These were acquired by A G Garrity who, after some difficulties over planning, developed the site. The arcade was completed late in 1956.

Fact File

During the building of the new sewer and the creation of the arcade, many artefacts were discovered which gave interesting insights to the town's past. These included part of the priory burial ground and a clay pipe kiln on the arcade site, and an old cobbler's shop near the Pavilion cinema which still had in it leather shoes from the 15th or 16th century.

The loss of supervised river bathing was keenly felt in the town and there was considerable local agitation for a swimming pool. Fund-raising for this made slow progress while costs rose rapidly. However, with the help of a substantial loan and grants, an open-air pool was built in Huntingdon Street in 1961. It proved to be very popular but was never financially secure, and its future often seemed uncertain. In 2004 age finally caught up with it and an unsatisfactory annual inspection led to its closure and subsequent demolition. An indoor pool had been built in Eynesbury in 1986, but for many this has been no substitute for the old, open-air pool.

The town also lacked a large modern venue for plays, concerts and similar events. There was, however, a suitable location available, rich in the town's history. This was the old priory site along by the river, no longer being used for industrial purposes. Initially it was hoped that the new hall could be built in the jubilee year of 1977 but the inevitable delays meant that the Priory Centre, as it was aptly named, did not open until December 1980.

Another part of the site was earmarked for a new library. There had been a branch library at St Neots since 1933, initially run by volunteers. The first purpose-built library had opened in Huntingdon Street in 1958, although it was 1962 before the town had a paid librarian. This library soon proved to be far too small for a fast-growing town, and the new, larger library, on the priory site, was eventually ready for opening in January 1985.

St Neots people had felt a great sense of deprivation for many years because the town did not have its own secondary school. This was eventually remedied with the building of what was initially a secondary modern school in 1959. It was decided that it should be called Longsands, the name by which the part of the town where it was built had been known for centuries, and it received its first intake in 1960. The school's status changed radically in 1965, when it was converted to become a comprehensive. A second comprehensive school followed in 1971 when Ernulf School

THE PRIORY CENTRE FROM THE TOWN BRIDGE
2005 S37713k (David Bushby)

(now St Neots Community College) was buil at Eynesbury, while new infant and junio schools, St Mary's and Priory, replaced out of-date 19th-century buildings.

Against the background of these nev facilities the plan was evolving that woulc dramatically change St Neots. The firs discussions with a number of Middlese boroughs regarding proposed overspil plans, which began in the early 1950s, were inconclusive, and in March 1959 it was learn that Ealing had decided against making any arrangement with St Neots. Agreement was reached, though, with three local authorities from Middlesex: Ruislip and Northwood District Council, Wood Green Corporation and Heston and Isleworth Corporation, and the first Middlesex families arrived in the town early in 1961. As the population continued to expand during the 1960s, house building pressed ahead rapidly and by Easter 1971 the construction of two thousand new council houses had been completed. Alongside this was a similar increase in private housing, including sites

HIGH STREET c1960 S37028

Dudeney & Johnson, Plums and the Three Tuns were all to go in sweeping changes along the High Street.

hat were made available for individuals who wanted to build their own homes.

Equally dramatic changes were occurring in the town centre. The 1960s brought the movement away from the traditional grocery stores towards more modern supermarkets. The first of these was in the St Neots Co-operative Society's High Street store. This opened in February 1962 and, in what was described at the time as 'fantastic opening trading', was taking nearly £1,000 a day. Not all shops shared in this boom and many traditional St Neots businesses closed. Plums had been a fixture in St Neots since 1814, and if you were in town in the afternoon, it was very much the accepted thing to have tea there. However, in 1976 the site was sold for redevelopment. John Rayns Smith,

which once claimed to hold the national record for prizes for its pork pies, was sold and subsequently closed in 1970. Boots and Iceland now occupy the sites of these two former St Neots institutions. W S Shepherd's bakery in South Street, where father and son between them had won more than 1,000 awards for bread and cakes, was also sold, in 1974.

Sadly, all these changes of the 1950s, 1960s and 1970s also involved the demolition of some of old St Neots. That of the cramped terraced houses in Russell Street in the late 1960s, as part of the council's slum clearance scheme, was not perhaps too much of a loss, but some important buildings also went. The warning signs were there in 1956 when Wisteria House, a fine 18th-century building in Huntingdon Street, was demolished to make way for a garage and car showrooms.

Priory Park and Priory Hill House, one-time home of the Rowley family, were acquired by the Urban District Council in 1964, and the house was subsequently demolished. Other buildings followed. The Pavilion closed in the declining years of the cinema in the late 1960s. It was demolished two years later, to be replaced by a block of shops and offices. The large Methodist chapel in Huntingdon Street was sold to the Co-op and demolished in 1972 to make room for an extension to its store.

Local government, too, saw an important change as Eaton Socon village and Eaton Ford were incorporated into the new, larger St Neots. The council was increased by five members to provide the Eatons with adequate representation, and the council chamber had to be extended to accommodate these new members in 1965.

There was also the necessary increase in industry, with firms like W R Grace and Kayser Bondor settling in the town. The paper mills, too, had once again become a major employer, having been acquired in 1950 by Samuel Jones Ltd. Extra land, the Island, was purchased in 1955 and a new factory extension was built in 1966. There was further expansion in 1971, and in 1972 a large paper-coating machine was installed. By 1974 the workforce had reached a considerable 800 in total.

Underlying all these developments there was a fundamental change taking place in the nature of St Neots. Its roots in agriculture, so

central for centuries, were being eroded, a were the core industries and family businesse that had long been the backbone of the town The town's position, near the A1 and with main-line railway link to London has mean that a significant part of its development ha: been as a commuter town, with increasing numbers of people working in Stevenage and London. In the 1960s St Neots station had only narrowly avoided falling victim to the notorious Beeching axe, and loca people were warned that if they did not use it, they would lose it. Now, following the electrification of the line in 1986, which ha: brought a fast through service to London, it i: one of the busiest stations on the line.

On the other side of things the cattle market, so important to the surrounding farming community for more than 100 years closed, with its final sale taking place on 2 March 1986. The site is now taken up by residential apartments, which have retained at least a memory of the past with the name of Old Market Court.

Fact File

For many years the cattle market had been run by Victor Ekins. During the Second World War he had been one of the fighter aces who had fought the Battle of Britain. In September 1940 his Hurricane had been shot down but, although badly wounded, he had managed to bale out to make a safe descent. He was awarded the Distinguished Flying Cross in June 1942.

NEW STREET c1955 S37003

The entrance to Ekins' Cattle Market can be seen on the right, just beyond the parked car.

Some of the old inns and public houses, which had been supported by members of the farming community, also closed. Most notable among these was the Cross Keys, which closed in November 1983. Fortunately, the façade has been retained and the Cross Keys now flourishes as a shopping mall.

In a rapidly changing world, other traditional St Neots businesses disappeared. The move to large brewery companies brought about the loss of Paines as a producer of beer in 1987, following a takeover of the business by Tollemache & Cobbold of Ipswich. This led to the extensive Paines' site on the Market Square standing empty and decaying for a decade. The sale of the local paper, the St Neots Advertiser, to the Cambridge Evening News Group of newspapers meant that the St Neots Advertiser building adjacent to it,

where the weekly paper had been printed for many years, was likewise to stand unused. After more than a century in the town the firm of C G Tebbutt closed in 1991, to be followed a few years later by the more recent Kayser Bondor. Both these sites have been redeveloped to provide new housing and have been given the names Navigation Wharf and Toller Mews - reminders of the days of the old river trade and of James Toller, the Eynesbury Giant.

Of all the losses that occurred in the last half of the 20th century, the one most keenly felt by many people was that of the old town bridge across the Ouse. In 1956 a hole appeared in the road surface and an inspection of the bridge revealed a serious structural defect. This led to restrictions being placed on traffic crossing the bridge. There was no money immediately available

The boarded-up shops behind the bus shelter are where the arcade was built in 1956. Beyond is the Cross Keys.

MARKET SQUARE c1955 S37005

THE BRIDGE AND BRIDGE HOTEL c1955 S37011

The Public Rooms can be seen above the parapet of the old bridge.

to remedy the problem, and it was only after years of one-way traffic and delays that it was replaced in 1964 by the present bridge. This also necessitated the demolition of the Public Rooms to provide the extra width that was needed for a temporary bridge. The new bridge improved the flow of the river, helping to ease, though by no means completely solve, the flooding problem that has so often plagued the town.

Near the old bridge there had been osie beds that had for many years sustained thriving basket-making industry. With it demise the osier beds were no longer neede and an ambitious plan set out to create riverside park as a major amenity for th town. This development began in April 197 and over a period of years the land alongsid the river was laid out with walks and tree and various leisure facilities.

The consulting architect for the new St Neots bridge was Sir Frederick Gibberd, CBE, famous as the designer of Harlow New Town, Heathrow Airport and Liverpool Metropolitan Cathedral. When he was interviewed on 'Desert Island Discs', he said that the St Neots bridge was the only one that he ever designed. It is listed among his major works in 'Who Was Who?'

THE BRIDGE c1965 S37065

THE RIVERSIDE PARK 2005 S37714k (David Bushby)

Fact File

In 1929 a house in River Terrace gained notoriety on account of the activities of a supposed poltergeist. Articles were mysteriously thrown around, much to the alarm of the adult members of the family who lived there. It has been suggested, though, that the whole thing was a clever hoax managed by their son!

RIVER TERRACE c1955 S37006

Facing onto the riverside park was the old River Terrace. In 1985 this was demolished and new, modern apartments built.

THE MODERN RIVER TERRACE 2005
S37715k (David Bushby)

For many years the St Neots Council had run the Thursday Market through a lease agreement with the Rowley family. This arrangement fell through in 1984 and it was leased instead to a private company. Fears were expressed at the time about the market's future but today it is one of the most flourishing in the area, attracting many visitors to the town each week.

MARKET SQUARE c1965 S37044

On days when there is no market the square is used extensively as a car park, although many people were unhappy with the introduction of a parking fee, combined with a limit on waiting time, in 1980.

Traffic congestion through Eaton Socon was eased when the A1 bypass opened in May 1971, but there was no such relief for St Neots. The tremendous increase in the volume of cars and lorries using the

fifteen-year period. It was 1984 before construction at last began and the St Neots bypass eventually opened on 20 December 1985, much to the relief of local people.

Meanwhile, the move from the traditional grocery stores to ever-larger supermarkets had continued, and in March 1987 a new Waitrose opened in the town. To accommodate the needs of shoppers, much of the remaining part of the priory site was laid out in a car park. Out-of-town shopping soon followed, with the Co-op opening its Rainbow store at Eaton in November 1991 and Tesco its store near the bypass at Eynesbury in June 1995. After some controversy, a Lidl store opened on the former Cedar House site in Cambridge Street in November 1998.

These out-of-town developments, with other economic factors, made the early 1990s difficult years for the town centre. There had been initial optimism when the old arcade had been replaced by the new Priory Mall shopping precinct in January 1990. However, this never flourished and by 1996 none of the shop units was occupied. Other shops in the town centre had also closed and it was claimed in 1995 that St Neots was fast becoming a ghost town.

main east-west route, which ran straight through the town, made St Neots a serious traffic bottleneck and a hazard for shoppers on the High Street. Campaigning for a bypass had faced many delays over a

MARKET SQUARE c1965 S37031

CHAPTER FIVE

A TOWN WITH A FUTURE

HIGH STREET c1955 S37024

THE YEARS of decline that had marked the first part of the 1990s were decisively reversed during the last years of the old century and the early years of the new millennium. The process of regeneration began with the redevelopment of the Market Square in 1997. Part of this work saw the restored Day Column moved on to a new, higher plinth which has given it greater prominence and made it much more of a feature.

The derelict buildings around the square, which had been the cause of grave concern, have also been brought back to life. After ten years of neglect the Paines' brewery site has been redeveloped in a mixed housing and business scheme. This began in 1998 and was completed in 2001. The old St Neots Advertiser building, too, has been restored and redeveloped and is now an Italian restaurant, while the main part of the failed Priory Mall has become the Priory restaurant and bar. Other empty properties in the town centre have once again been occupied and town centre manager, David Gregory, was able to claim in January 2002 that St Neots was 'firing on all cylinders'.

The years since the millennium have seen various moves to enhance the town's facilities. The disappearance of the Jubilee

Clock had long been a matter of contention and debate. In the year 2000 the Rotary Club of St Neots decided to celebrate the millennium with the gift of a new clock to the town, and this now hangs on the side of Brittains' furniture store in the High Street.

The need for additional leisure facilities had long been recognised and an important move in this direction came with the opening of the Eat 'N' Bowl bowling alley in Huntingdon Street in August 2001.

THE ROTARY CLUB MILLENNIUM CLOCK 2005
S37716k (David Bushby)

EAT 'N' BOWL BOWLING ALLEY 2001 S37717k (David Bushby)

A VIEW OF THE TOWN

The best way to see the pattern of today's St Neots is to climb the church tower on one of those occasions on summer Saturdays when it is open. It is not an easy climb up the worn and winding steps, but the panorama of the town and distant countryside spread out in all directions makes it well worth the effort.

THE VIEW FROM THE CHURCH TOWER 2005
S37718k (David Bushby)

The view from St Neots Church tower, looking north towards the common.

Some of the most notable developments of the new millennium have taken place at the Eynesbury end of the town. These have included the enlargement of the Tesco store near the bypass, the reconstruction of the road bridge over Hen Brook in St Mary's Street, and a large new housing complex and marina on land off Barford Road.

This development includes a new concept in residential care with the building of Poppyfields by Hanover Housing Association. Here residents have their own flats, so retaining their independence, but also have the security of knowing that there is 24-hour care available.

Another important aspect of this development is a new park, and this forms part of a wider vision to improve access to, and the environment of, the whole of the green wedge that runs through the centre of St Neots from Little Barford to Little Paxton.

At the Little Paxton end of St Neots, many of the old buildings on the paper mills site, rendered redundant by a marked decline in business there during the 1990s, were demolished in 2002 and further residential and community development is in progress there.

Future plans for St Neots are ambitious and far-reaching. These include substantial redevelopment in the Longsands area and also around St Neots Community College in Eynesbury, providing new leisure and community facilities. Plans are well advanced for extensive residential development east of the railway line off the Cambridge road, and included in this scheme will be new and improved facilities for St Neots Football Club, an all-weather pitch, indoor sports facilities, a primary school and a local centre. A new bridge across the Ouse to facilitate the movement of cyclists and pedestrians between Eynesbury and Eaton Socon is also envisaged. It is further hoped that a long-standing scheme for a new community centre at Eaton Socon will come to fruition in 2006.

Beyond these individual schemes there is a 'Vision for St Neots' compiled for Huntingdon District Council by the Civic Trust in consultation with St Neots Town Council and other interested bodies. This will impact on all the areas in the older parts of the town, improving and enhancing facilities and, in particular helping to ensure the continued vitality and viability of the town centre. All these schemes mark a determination to make St Neots not only the largest town in Cambridgeshire but also the best and one of which all who live in it can feel proud.

POPPYFIELDS 2005 S37719k (David Bushby)

ACKNOWLEDGEMENTS

Most of the material used in this book has come from three important local sources: the Huntingdon Record Office, St Neots Library, and the Norris Museum at St Ives. I am grateful to all those staff who have found me material and answered my questions. I am especially indebted to Bob Burn-Murdock at the Norris Museum for his help with illustrations and ephemera. I would also thank Mr Malcolm Sharp, Head of Planning Services at Huntingdonshire District Council, for helping me with information about future plans for St Neots.

My knowledge of the history of St Neots has been built up over the last 38 years and I am indebted to a number of people for the help they have given me. Foremost among these was the late Leslie Forscutt, whose knowledge of the town was unparalleled. I also owe a great deal to Ken Barringer, George Casson, Bert Goodwin, David Rudd and Rosa Young, all of whom have made significant contributions.

There have been several other people who have provided me with helpful information and material and I am grateful to them. These are Alan Butler, Roger Day, Ron Dyer and Jean Hawkins.

BIBLIOGRAPHY

The History and Antiquities of Eynesbury and St Neots - George Cornelius Gorham (1820 and 1824)
St Neots: the History of a Huntingdonshire Town - C G Tebbutt (1978 and 1984)
St Neots Past - Rosa Young (1996)
St Neots Urban District Council, 1894 - 1974 Peter Brice and others (1974)
St Neots in Old Picture Postcards (1) - Rosa Young
St Neots in Old Picture Postcards (2) - Rosa Young
The Chronicles of the Rowleys - Peter Rowley (1995)
St Neots Priory - David Rudd (2004)
St Neots Local History Society Magazine, Nos 1 - 60 (bound copies are available in the reference section of St Neots Library).
Local Newspapers:
The Cambridge Chronicle
The St Neots Chronicle
The St Neots Advertiser

Future plans for St Neots can be found on the Huntingdonshire District Council website, www.huntsdc.gov.uk/planning.

FRITH PRODUCTS & SERVICES

Francis Frith would doubtless be pleased to know that the pioneering publishing venture he started in 1860 still continues today. Over a hundred and forty years later, The Francis Frith Collection continues in the same innovative tradition and is now one of the foremost publishers of vintage photographs in the world. Some of the current activities include:

INTERIOR DECORATION

Today Frith's photographs can be seen framed and as giant wall murals in thousands of pubs, restaurants, hotels, banks, retail stores and other public buildings throughout the country. In every case they enhance the unique local atmosphere of the places they depict and provide reminders of gentler days in an increasingly busy and frenetic world.

PRODUCT PROMOTIONS

Frith products are used by many major companies to promote the sales of their own products or to reinforce their own history and heritage. Frith promotions have been used by Hovis bread, Courage beers, Scots Porage Oats, Colman's mustard, Cadbury's foods, Mellow Birds coffee, Dunhill pipe tobacco, Guinness, and Bulmer's Cider.

GENEALOGY AND FAMILY HISTORY

As the interest in family history and roots grows world-wide, more and more people are turning to Frith's photographs of Great Britain for images of the towns, villages and streets where their ancestors lived; and, of course, photographs of the churches and chapels where their ancestors were christened, married and buried are an essential part of every genealogy tree and family album.

FRITH PRODUCTS

All Frith photographs are available Framed or just as Mounted Prints and Posters (size 23 x 16 inches). These may be ordered from the address below. Other products available are - Address Books, Calendars, Jigsaws, Canvas Prints, Postcards and local and prestige books.

THE INTERNET

Already ninety thousand Frith photographs can be viewed and purchased on the internet through the Frith websites and a myriad of partner sites.

For more detailed information on Frith products, look at this site:
www.francisfrith.com

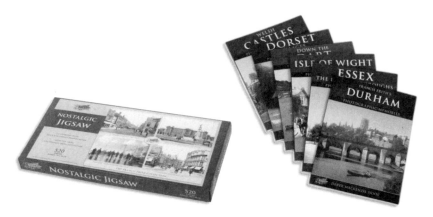

See the complete list of Frith Books at: www.francisfrith.com
This web site is regularly updated with the latest list of publications from The Francis Frith Collection. If you wish to buy books relating to another part of the country that your local bookshop does not stock, you may purchase on-line.

For further information, trade, or author enquiries please contact us at the address below:
The Francis Frith Collection, Unit 6, Oakley Business Park, Wylye Road, Dinton, Wiltshire SP3 5EU.
Tel: +44 (0)1722 716 376 Fax: +44 (0)1722 716 881 Email: sales@francisfrith.co.uk

See Frith products on the internet at www.francisfrith.com

FREE PRINT OF YOUR CHOICE
CHOOSE A PHOTOGRAPH FROM THIS BOOK

+ £3.50 POSTAGE

Mounted Print
Overall size 14 x 11 inches (355 x 280mm)

TO RECEIVE YOUR FREE PRINT

Choose any Frith photograph in this book

Simply complete the Voucher opposite and return it with your remittance for £3.50 (to cover postage and handling) and we will print the photograph of your choice in SEPIA (size 11 x 8 inches) and supply it in a cream mount ready to frame (overall size 14 x 11 inches).

Order additional Mounted Prints
at HALF PRICE - £10.00 each (normally £20.00)

If you would like to order more Frith prints from this book, possibly as gifts for friends and family, you can buy them at half price (with no additional postage costs).

Have your Mounted Prints framed

For an extra £19.00 per print you can have your mounted print(s) framed in an elegant polished wood and gilt moulding, overall size 16 x 13 inches (no additional postage required).

IMPORTANT!

❶ Please note: aerial photographs and photographs with a reference number starting with a "Z" are not Frith photographs and cannot be supplied under this offer.

❷ Offer valid for delivery to one UK address only.

❸ These special prices are only available if you use this form to order. You must use the ORIGINAL VOUCHER on this page (no copies permitted). We can only despatch to one UK address.

❹ This offer cannot be combined with any other offer.

As a customer your name & address will be stored by Frith but not sold or rented to third parties. Your data will be used for the purpose of this promotion only.

Send completed Voucher form to:

**The Francis Frith Collection,
6 Oakley Business Park, Wylye Road,
Dinton, Wiltshire SP3 5EU**

Voucher for **FREE** and *Reduced Price Frith Prints*

Please do not photocopy this voucher. Only the original is valid, so please fill it in, cut it out and return it to us with your order.

Picture ref no	Page no	Qty	Mounted @ £10.00	Framed + £19.50	Total Cost £
		1	Free of charge*	£	£
			£10.00	£	£
			£10.00	£	£
			£10.00	£	£
			£10.00	£	£
			£10.00	£	£

Please allow 28 days for delivery. Offer available to one UK address only

* Post & handling	£3.80
Total Order Cost	£

Title of this book . . . .

I enclose a cheque/postal order for £ . . . . made payable to 'The Francis Frith Collection'

OR please debit my Mastercard / Visa / Maestro card, details below

Card Number:

Issue No (Maestro only):   Valid from (Maestro):

Card Security Number: Expires:

Signature:

Name Mr/Mrs/Ms . . . .

Address . . . .

. . . .

. . . .

. . . . Postcode . . . .

Daytime Tel No . . . .

Email . . . .

Valid to 31/12/15

Free Print – see overleaf

Can you help us with information about any of the Frith photographs in this book?

We are gradually compiling an historical record for each of the photographs in the Frith archive. It is always fascinating to find out the names of the people shown in the pictures, as well as insights into the shops, buildings and other features depicted.

If you recognize anyone in the photographs in this book, or if you have information not already included in the author's caption, do let us know. We would love to hear from you, and will try to publish it in future books or articles.

An Invitation from The Francis Frith Collection to Share Your Memories

The 'Share Your Memories' feature of our website allows members of the public to add personal memories relating to the places featured in our photographs, or comment on others already added. Seeing a place from your past can rekindle forgotten or long held memories. Why not visit the website, find photographs of places you know well and add YOUR story for others to read and enjoy? We would love to hear from you!

www.francisfrith.com/memories

Our production team

Frith books are produced by a small dedicated team at offices near Salisbury. Most have worked with the Frith Collection for many years. All have in common one quality: they have a passion for the Frith Collection.

Frith Books and Gifts

We have a wide range of books and gifts available on our website utilising our photographic archive, many of which can be individually personalised.

www.francisfrith.com